The Prince
Interpreted for Content Creators

Maintaining Power, Loyalty, and Authority as Your Audience Grows

---

ANCIENT WISDOM HACKS

Publisher: NX Inc

Third Edition

Contents

Chapter 3: Alliances and Networks
• Strategic Partnerships: Collaborations, Guest Posts, and Co-Streams
• Influencer Diplomacy: Balancing Give-and-Take
• Community Building: Forums, Discords, and Centralized Hubs
• Action Steps: Outreach Email Scripts; Partnership Scorecard

---

Part II: Crafting Your Image

Chapter 4: The Art of Perception Management
• Curating Your Persona: Authenticity vs. Aspiration
• Visual Consistency: Thumbnails, Color Palettes, and Logos
• Storytelling as Spin: Positioning Your Narrative
• Action Steps: Brand Style Guide; Narrative Storyboard

Chapter 5: Reputation and Credibility
• Machiavellian Reputation Tactics: Praise, Blame, and Selective Disclosure
• Social Proof: Testimonials, Reviews, and User-Generated Content
• Handling Crisis: Apology vs. Pivot Strategies
• Action Steps: Reputation Tracker; Crisis Response Flowchart

Chapter 6: The Power of Surprise and Innovation
• Disruption Over Convention: Case Studies of Viral Pivots
• Timing and Rhythm: When to Launch Bold Experiments
• Balancing "Fresh" with "Familiar": A/B Testing for Creatives
• Action Steps: Innovation Sprint Plan; Testing Matrix

Part III: Strategy in Action

Chapter 7: Competitive Analysis

- Mapping Rival Creators: Strengths, Weaknesses, and Openings
- SWOT for Content Strategies
- Blue-Ocean Content: Finding Uncontested Niches
- Action Steps: Competitor Map; Blue-Ocean Brainstorming

Chapter 8: Resource Management
- Time, Tools, and Team: Budgeting Your Resources Wisely
- Outsourcing vs. In-House: Freelancers, Agencies, and Interns
- Scaling Content Operations Without Diluting Quality
- Action Steps: Resource Allocation Worksheet; ROI Calculator

Chapter 9: Tactical Promotion and Distribution
- Organic Reach vs. Paid Amplification
- Platforms Triage: When to Double Down or Pull Back
- Cross-Platform Repurposing: Maximizing ROI on Each Asset
- Action Steps: Channel Decision Narrative; Repurposing Checklist

Chapter 10: Monetization and Revenue Streams
- Direct (Ads, Sponsorships) vs. Indirect (Merch, Courses) Models
- Subscriptions, Memberships, and Patreon Mechanics
- Pricing Psychology: Fees, Tiers, and Perceived Value
- Action Steps: Monetization Roadmap; Pricing Tier Worksheet

Part IV: Sustaining Success

Chapter 11: Adaptation and Resilience
• Reading Platform Signals and Algorithm Shifts
• Pivot Frameworks: When and How to Change Direction
• Building Redundancy: Diversifying Content and Income
• Action Steps: Scenario Planning; Stress-Test Your Strategy

Chapter 12: Legacy and Long-Term Influence
• Thought Leadership: Writing Books, Speaking Engagements, and Courses
• Mentorship and Community Stewardship
• Preparing Exit Strategies: Selling, Handing Off, or Retiring Your Brand
• Action Steps: Legacy Blueprint; Mentee Program Outline

Conclusion and Next Steps
• Review of Core Lessons
• Creating Your Personal "Prince's Plan"

- Guided Template to Map Strategy, Actions, and Checkpoints
  • Staying the Course

- Encouragement for Ongoing Adaptation and Growth
  • Final Reflective Prompts for Vision and Mission Alignment

---

Introduction

Purpose and Scope
This book exists to translate the razor-sharp insights of
Machiavelli's *The Prince* into a playbook for today's content
creators. Just as Machiavelli dissected the mechanics of power in
16th-century Italy, we'll dissect the mechanics of influence in the
age of TikTok, podcasts, and personal brands. We'll pull apart his
core arguments—about perception, reputation, alliances, and
adaptability—and rebuild them around subscriber counts,
engagement rates, and platform algorithms.

Why Machiavelli Matters to Modern Content Creators
Creators live in a realm of constant competition: everyone is vying
for attention, loyalty, and trust. Machiavelli understood that, to
thrive, a leader must master both the art of persuasion and the art
of action. He wrote, "It is much safer to be feared than loved,
when, of the two, either must be lacking." In our world, that
translates into knowing when to push bold opinions and when to
lean into consensus. He reminds us that authenticity without
strategy is reckless—and strategy without authenticity is hollow.
By following his pragmatic, results-driven approach, you'll learn
when to charm your audience and when to command it.

From Renaissance Courts to Digital Platforms: A Brief Bridge
Imagine the princely courts of Florence, where every move was
calculated for maximum advantage. Now swap palaces for
platforms: YouTube channels replace court factions, algorithms
replace alliances, and comments sections replace diplomatic
audiences. Machiavelli's advice on surveying terrain, building
coalitions, and pivoting in response to betrayal becomes advice on

reading analytics, forging collaborations, and responding to algorithm changes. Though the courtly rituals have changed, the underlying dynamics of influence remain the same.

How to Use This Book
 The journey here unfolds in three steps: **Lessons** ⇒ **Strategy** ⇒ **Action.** Each chapter begins with a timeless lesson drawn directly from *The Prince*. Next, we translate that lesson into a concrete strategy tailored for digital creators. Finally, you get a hands-on Action section—step-by-step prompts you can implement immediately.

Throughout, you'll find reflective exercises and "creator's journal" prompts to anchor each insight in your own experience. Use them to plan your next campaign, assess your reputation metrics, or prototype a bold new experiment. By the end of these ten pages, you'll not only understand why Machiavelli's advice still cuts deep—you'll know exactly how to wield it in your own creator journey.

Chapter 1: Establishing Your Domain

Defining Your Niche: The Modern Princedom

In *The Prince*, Machiavelli emphasizes the importance of securing and holding a territory that you can call your own. He writes, "A prince ought to have no other aim or thought, nor take up any other thing for his study, but war and its organization and discipline…" In our world of content creation, "war" becomes the battle for attention, and the "territory" is your niche. To stand out amid the endless din, you must choose a domain narrow enough to dominate, yet broad enough to sustain growth.

Begin by surveying the landscape of content: list the areas you know well, from personal passion points to professional expertise. Don't default to the most crowded fields—rather, look for where your unique combination of skills, stories, and perspectives can fill a gap. As Machiavelli tells us, acquiring a new principality is hardest of all, yet "those who acquire it by ability have the support of all who profit by their winnings." If you define your niche by genuine skill and enthusiasm, you'll attract an audience that rallies around your authority.

Next, consider how your background and experience shape your domain. A prince who rules in lands he has known since childhood enjoys an advantage; he understands the customs and the loyalties. Likewise, your personal history—your education, your career detours, your travels—gives you access to a particular audience. Own those markers of authenticity. If you spent years as a nonprofit fundraiser before pivoting to video essays, let that shape your niche around storytelling with purpose.

Finally, set clear boundaries for your niche. Machiavelli warns against overextending one's resources, advising princes to consolidate gains before seeking new conquests. Similarly, define the scope of your content: what themes you will cover, what formats you'll master, and which platforms you'll dominate. Write down a mission statement: "I am the go-to creator for…" Use it as your north star. When brand partnerships tempt you into unrelated topics, refer back to this core statement and refuse to stray.

Assessing Audience Terrain: Demographics vs. Psychographics

Machiavelli counsels princes to know their people: their fears, their hopes, and the local customs. He observes, "He who becomes prince through the favour of the people ought to keep them friendly by satisfying them." In the creator economy, satisfying your audience means tailoring content that resonates not just with who they are, but with why they care.

Start by mapping demographics: age brackets, locations, languages, education levels. These data points form the broad contours of your domain. Yet just as Machiavelli warns that understanding geography alone is insufficient, demographics alone won't secure loyalty. The greater advantage comes from psychographics—your audience's values, aspirations, pain points, and lifestyle choices.

Conduct surveys or choose two or three core fans and interview them. Ask about their daily routines: when do they find time to consume content, and in what context? What frustrations are they seeking to alleviate—boredom on a commute, loneliness in a new city, confusion around a skill they wish to learn? As Machiavelli notes that men are moved more by "love and reverence" when they share needs, you'll forge stronger bonds by addressing emotional drivers.

Segment your tribe into "courtiers," "subjects," and "allies." Courtiers are superfans who actively comment, share, and create fan art. Subjects consume passively but consistently. Allies—other creators or industry voices—can amplify your message when aligned. Tailor content types to each: exclusive behind-the-scenes for courtiers; evergreen tutorials for subjects; collaborative livestreams for allies.

Regularly revisit this terrain map. Just as princes must adapt to shifting loyalties, your audience's preferences evolve. Use analytics to spot trends—an uptick in mobile views might prompt shorter, snackable clips. Look for dips in watch time as signals that you need to recalibrate. Keep your ear to the ground through community polls, direct messages, and social listening.

First Impressions: Profile, Branding, and the All-Important Bio

Machiavelli understood that a prince's reputation is shaped as much by initial gestures as by long-term deeds: "Men judge generally more by the eye than by the hand." In the digital realm, your profile picture, banner, and bio line are that "eye" through which newcomers form split-second opinions.

Begin with your visual identity. Choose a profile image where you appear confident and approachable—eye contact with the lens, a setting that hints at your niche (a microphone for podcasters, a sketchpad for illustrators). For your banner or header graphic, incorporate a bold color palette and minimal typography that echoes your personality. Keep it clutter-free: viewers should instantly know what to expect when they land on your page.

Next, craft a bio that hits three notes: who you are, what you do, and why it matters. Machiavelli extols brevity in proclamations—"A prince ought to appear to be merciful, faithful, humane, upright, and religious…" Yet space is limited. Your bio might read: "Data analyst turned storytelling podcaster. I break down complex insights into 10-minute episodes that spark real change." That single sentence positions you as expert, format specialist, and solution provider.

Don't neglect SEO. Sprinkle one or two keywords naturally within your bio—words your ideal audience is likely to search. If your domain is "zero-waste cooking," make sure that phrase appears verbatim. This is your chance to seize the first page of search results before competitors claim it.

Finally, synchronize your branding across platforms. Machiavelli warns against changing methods mid-campaign; inconsistency breeds suspicion. Whether on YouTube, Instagram, or TikTok, use the same photo, handle, and core messaging. A visitor should look at your Twitter and instantly recognize it's the same "prince" they encountered on LinkedIn or your blog.

Action Steps: Niche Worksheet; Brand Audit

Niche Worksheet

1. List five areas where you hold unique expertise or passion.

2. For each area, note your potential audience size and saturation level (high/medium/low).

3. Select the top two areas and write a one-sentence niche statement for each: "I am the go-to creator for ________."

4. Choose one statement that feels both narrow and sustainable. Commit to it for the next 90 days.

Brand Audit

1. Screenshot your profile on each active platform. Evaluate:

   - Visual consistency (photo, colors, fonts)

- Bio clarity (who, what, why)

- Keyword presence

2. Rate each profile on a scale of 1–5 for first-impression impact.

3. Identify one platform where your branding feels weakest. Rewrite the bio and update the visuals there this week.

4. Share the updated profile with a trusted peer or follower and solicit feedback: what did they understand in the first five seconds?

By completing these exercises, you'll emerge with a clearly defined principality in the content landscape, an intimate map of your audience's desires, and a polished front door that invites newcomers into your realm. With your domain secured, you're ready to move on to building authority and forging alliances—just as Machiavelli's princes did before you.

Chapter 2: Building and Maintaining Authority

Authority vs. Popularity: Lessons from Hereditary vs. New Princes

Machiavelli opens *The Prince* with a stark comparison: those born to rule enjoy the stability of long-standing dynasties, while newcomers must fight every step of the way. He writes, "Princedoms which have been accustomed to live under their own laws [hereditary princedoms]… are less difficult to hold than new ones." New princes, he warns, "must, in order to preserve themselves, establish new laws and new taxes; and these… cannot be established without the people's discontent."

For content creators, hereditary princes are the established stars—those who inherit built-in audiences through family businesses, celebrity status, or long careers. A YouTube scion taking over a parent's channel, or an actor turning to livestreams, begins with viewers predisposed to trust. In contrast, the new prince is the garage podcaster, the first-generation blogger, or the social-media novice: authority must be carved from scratch.

Popularity—viral hits, trending hashtags, celebrity shout-outs—can feel like instant power. Yet Machiavelli reminds us that popularity is fickle: "Men change their ruler… when they find themselves oppressed by his taxes or ill-treatment." If your entire influence rests on fleeting trends or borrowed fame, you risk losing it the moment the algorithm shifts or a sponsor departs. True authority, by contrast, is deeper; it's the hard-won respect of an audience that values your expertise, your integrity, and your consistent delivery of value.

To bridge the gap between popularity and authority, a new creator must focus relentlessly on competence. Just as Machiavelli counsels princes to draw support by "the virtue of their ability," so must you showcase your mastery. Publish tutorials that solve real problems, host interviews that reveal insider knowledge, and share personal stories that underscore your lived experience. With each piece of content, you convert casual viewers into loyal subjects.

Consistency, Frequency, and Style: Your "Currency"

In Renaissance Italy, princely coffers needed steady income to pay mercenaries and fund fortifications. For modern creators, your coffers are the algorithmic favor, audience goodwill, and partnership opportunities you accumulate day by day. Machiavelli might liken consistency, frequency, and style to the steady tribute a principality pays: skip a payment, and loyalty might waver.

- **Consistency**: Aligns your audience's expectations. Machiavelli writes that a prince "must not touch the property or the women of his citizens," preserving trust. Likewise, if you promise weekly deep-dives or daily motivational posts, breaking that promise erodes confidence. Viewers start to expect—and then to miss—you.

- **Frequency**: Fuels the algorithm. Just as a prince must appear frequently before his courtiers to maintain rapport, you must show up in feeds. Each upload, tweet, or story is a small tribute that reminds the algorithm—and your audience—that you're active, relevant, and deserving of attention.

- **Style**: Distinguishes you from rivals. Machiavelli emphasizes that a prince should cultivate a persona: "it is necessary… to seem merciful, faithful, humane, upright, and religious." Your style—your thumbnails, your tone of voice, your editing quirks—communicates your brand values at a glance. It's the uniform your troops recognize instantly.

Viewed together, these three form your creator currency. Spend it wisely: overproduce low-quality posts, and you dilute your authority. Post infrequently, and you risk being forgotten. Copy another creator's style, and you become interchangeable. Instead, aim for a sustainable rhythm—one that balances quality with quantity—anchored by a style uniquely yours.

Handling Trolls and Negative Feedback: Turning Critics into Allies

"No enterprise is more likely to succeed than one concealed from the enemy until it can be executed with all its forces," Machiavelli advises princes planning clandestine operations. While you needn't hide your flaws, there is wisdom in choosing when and how to confront criticism. Trolls and negative comments are inevitable. Your task is to turn friction into fuel.

First, understand motivations. Some trolls seek attention; others are testing your resolve or championing a different perspective. Before reacting, pause and assess: is this a chance to clarify a misunderstanding, or is it a bait-and-switch designed to spark drama? Machiavelli warns that princes who respond hastily to every insult find themselves perpetually distracted from governance. The same holds true for creators: defending every slight can derail your focus.

Second, choose your battlefield. Publicly defusing a genuine concern shows transparency and confidence: "I appreciate your feedback; let me explain how I came to this conclusion…" This approach often converts skeptics into curious followers. Conversely, if a comment is simply toxic, take the discussion offline. Offer a private message or email: "Let's discuss this further away from the public thread." Often, the critic will either apologize or vanish, and you avoid giving them the spotlight.

Third, mine for insight. Machiavelli notes that "the vulgar crowd always is taken by appearances," yet "the wise are judged by their deeds." Treat negative feedback as reconnaissance: patterns in criticism can reveal blind spots in your content, gaps in your communication, or unmet audience needs. Use these insights to refine future uploads. Show your audience you listen by completely overhauling a format, clarifying confusing terminology, or addressing a missed story angle.

Finally, reward constructive criticism. Create a monthly spotlight post that highlights the most insightful viewer suggestions. Invite critics to guest-co-create content or lead Q&A sessions. By elevating them, you demonstrate that authority isn't a shield against dissent but a platform for collaborative growth. Over time, you'll find that turning critics into allies not only neutralizes negativity but also expands your loyal cadre.

Action Steps: Content Calendar Template; Feedback Protocol

1. Content Calendar Template

- **Weekly Themes**: Assign each week a thematic focus aligned with your niche (e.g., "Beginner's Bootcamp," "Advanced Tactics," "Case Studies").

- **Daily Format Slots**: Block out formats for each weekday (e.g., Monday written post, Tuesday short video, Wednesday live stream, Thursday infographic, Friday roundup).

- **Strategic Milestones**: Mark dates for launches, collaborations, and sponsored content. Ensure spacing to avoid audience fatigue.

- **Review Checkpoints**: Every two weeks, review metrics: engagement rates, watch time, and audience growth. Adjust the next period's calendar accordingly.

2. Feedback Protocol

- **Categorize Comments**: Create three folders—"Praise," "Questions/Misunderstandings," "Critiques." Automate comment exports weekly.

- **Response Guidelines**:

  1. *Praise*: Thank personally or publicly; encourage sharing.

  2. *Questions*: Address in upcoming content or a dedicated FAQ segment.

  3. *Critiques*: Evaluate for validity; file actionable items for your next content iteration.

- **Escalation Ladder**: For repeat offenders or potential trolls:

  1. Private reply offering to discuss offline.

  2. Temporary comment moderation if toxicity persists.

3. Block or mute only if all else fails—preserving community safety.

- **Recognition Ritual**: At month-end, highlight the top three constructive suggestions in a "Viewer Voice" segment. Credit contributors visibly.

By mastering the balance between authority and popularity, maintaining the steady flow of high-quality content, and transforming criticism into a co-creative force, you build an unshakeable principality in the digital realm. Like Machiavelli's ideal prince, your power will stem not from fleeting applause, but from the respect of a community that knows, trusts, and rallies behind you.

Chapter 3: Alliances and Networks

In *The Prince*, Machiavelli underscores that no ruler governs in isolation. Even the mightiest need allies to secure borders, supply arms, and legitimize authority. He warns against overreliance on mercenaries or auxiliary forces, yet he also teaches that shrewd partnerships can cement power more durably than solitary conquest. "He who becomes prince through the favour of the people ought to keep them friendly by satisfying them," he writes, and later reminds us that "a prince must lay foundations on which his state may rest securely." For content creators, alliances—through collaborations, guest posts, co-streams, and community hubs—serve as those very foundations. In this chapter, we translate Machiavellian counsel into actionable guidance for forging relationships that expand reach, reinforce credibility, and protect against the volatility of solo ventures.

Strategic Partnerships: Collaborations, Guest Posts, and Co-Streams

Machiavelli devotes significant attention to the military alliances of his day—how princes recruit mercenary bands, when they summon auxiliary troops from neighboring rulers, and why both methods ultimately risk betrayal or dependence. He warns that "auxiliaries are useless and dangerous," for they are loyal not to the prince but to their own sovereign. Yet he also recognizes that skilled generals sometimes deploy mercenaries with great success, provided they guard against overdependence.

Translated to content creation, this means that strategic partnerships—collaborations with fellow creators, guest posts on established blogs, and co-streams on each other's channels—can turbocharge your growth, but only if entered with clear terms, mutual benefit, and exit strategies. Like a prince vetting a military captain, you must assess potential collaborators on competence, alignment, and reliability.

1. **Identify Complementary Strengths**

   - Map your own assets—your niche expertise, production quality, storytelling flair—and seek partners whose strengths fill your gaps. If you excel at long-form interviews but struggle with short-form video, team up with a TikTok storyteller. If you have deep subject-matter knowledge but lack design chops, guest-post on a visual art blog that can elevate your written essays.

   - Machiavelli advises choosing generals who have both virtu (skill) and fama (reputation). Similarly, partner with creators whose portfolios demonstrate consistent excellence and whose audiences trust their recommendations.

2. **Define Mutual Objectives**

   - Before you record a podcast together or exchange guest posts, clarify goals: is it audience growth, brand awareness, product co-development, or lead generation? Write a simple one-page partnership brief outlining each party's deliverables, timelines, and success metrics.

- By formalizing expectations, you avoid the fate of princes who lose support through misunderstandings or shifting loyalties.

3. **Negotiate Equitable Terms**

- Machiavelli counsels that a prudent prince "ought to seem merciful, faithful, humane, upright, and religious." In negotiations, be transparent about what you offer and what you request. If your collaborator brings a 100K email list, and you bring a 50K subscriber base, consider revenue-share splits, cross-promotional commitments, or equity in co-branded products that reflect that imbalance.

- Document intellectual-property rights, exclusivity windows, and attribution language. Even prolific medieval dukes signed charters; you should sign a Google Doc.

4. **Structure Phased Commitments**

- Rather than plunging into an expansive co-course or multi-episode series, begin with a smaller pilot: a single co-stream or a guest blog. This "mercenary scouting party" approach lets you test chemistry, workflow, and audience response before doubling down.

- If initial results satisfy both sides, escalate to deeper integrations—a co-produced ebook, a joint webinar series, or a shared Patreon tier.

5. **Maintain Independence While Leveraging Synergy**

   - Machiavelli warns that princes must guard their autonomy: "He who relies entirely on good faith is often deceived." Never cede full control over your brand or content. Retain sole editorial authority, and use partnerships to amplify—not absorb—your voice.

   - Keep your own content pipeline flowing in parallel. Even as you co-stream weekly, maintain your solo uploads so that your audience never associates your output exclusively with the partnership.

6. **Exit with Dignity**

   - All alliances have a lifespan. Circumstances change: an algorithm update, a market shift, or divergent creative visions. Plan an amicable exit by embedding a review point after three months. If either party feels the value isn't mutual, wind down with gratitude, publicly thanking one another for the journey. This preserves goodwill for future ventures.

By treating collaborations as strategic military counsel—selecting skilled allies, defining clear objectives, and preserving autonomy—you build a network that reinforces your authority without entangling you in dependency.

Influencer Diplomacy: Balancing Give-and-Take

In his analysis of interstate diplomacy, Machiavelli highlights the importance of reciprocity. Princes exchanged ambassadors, gifts, and even royal marriages to cement ties. However, he cautions that a wise ruler "ought never to keep faith when by doing so it would be against his interests," emphasizing that diplomatic generosity must always serve the state's core security.

For creators, influencer diplomacy is the art of exchanging value with peers and industry leaders—whether through shout-outs, joint campaigns, or cross-promotions—while safeguarding your brand's long-term interests.

1. **Assess the Power Dynamics**

   - Before approaching a larger influencer for a mention or collaboration, gauge relative audience size, engagement rates, and brand fit. If the imbalance is extreme, propose low-risk mutual benefits: perhaps you contribute a guest segment to their live show in exchange for a single-line endorsement at the end.

   - Machiavelli notes that "men are driven by two principal impulses, either by love or by fear." In influencer relationships, a smaller creator often courts favor through goodwill—providing exclusive insights or bespoke content—hoping to inspire "love." Larger influencers respond to either genuine enthusiasm or tangible gain (their own "fear" of missing out). Tailor your approach accordingly.

2. **Cultivate a Gift Economy**

   - Send thoughtful resources: a well-researched case study, an invite to an off-record mastermind, or early access to a beta tool. These gestures cost you relatively little time or money but can win significant loyalty.

   - Document your offerings: keep a spreadsheet—private and confidential—of whom you've gifted what, and monitor any shifts in engagement or responsiveness.

3. **Negotiate Reciprocity**

   - When requesting a favor—be it a tweet, a feature, or an introduction—frame it as part of a broader mutual exchange. Say, "I'd love your feedback on my upcoming series; in return, I can amplify your next product launch to my 20K subscribers." This "you scratch my back" dynamic echoes Machiavelli's insight that alliances solidify most when both parties perceive clear, balanced advantage.

4. **Manage Expectations Precisely**

   - Set concrete deliverables: "One Instagram story, three tweets, and a newsletter mention, all within 30 days of launch." Avoid vague promises like "help me out next week." Clear timelines mirror the contracts princes used to bind each other.

5. **Monitor and Adapt to Shifts**

   - Just as political alliances fracture when one side grows too powerful, influencer ties can sour if one account outpaces the other dramatically. Regularly review web analytics and social metrics. If the balance swings heavily, renegotiate terms: request additional shout-outs, propose deeper content swaps, or gently wind down the partnership.

6. **Protect Against Bad Faith**

   - Machiavelli warns that "men are ungrateful, fickle, liars, and deceivers." Keep copies of all agreements, track actual versus promised promotions, and be prepared to publicly thank allies—but privately move on if they fail to deliver. Never issue an ultimatum; instead, let a lack of reciprocity naturally diminish future overtures.

Through disciplined diplomacy—strategic generosity paired with shrewd safeguarding of your interests—you cultivate a network of influencers who boost your reach without undermining your independence.

Community Building: Forums, Discords, and Centralized Hubs

Machiavelli taught that a prince's true power lies in the loyalty of his subjects. In chapter 9, he observes that "men are excited more by the need to conform than by free will," and in chapter 19 he warns that nobles often rebel when they feel excluded from power. Translating this into the creator sphere, your community—whether gathered on your website's forum, a private Discord server, or an email list—becomes the bedrock of sustained influence.

1. **Choose Your Stronghold**

   - Select a platform that aligns with your audience's habits and comfort level. For a technical, niche community, a forum on your own domain may work best; for younger, chat-centric users, Discord or Slack could be ideal. Email lists remain the most sovereign territory, immune to platform algorithm changes.

   - Machiavelli reminds princes that fortress walls protect from external invasion. Likewise, hosting your community on your own domain ensures you're not evicted by sudden policy shifts on third-party platforms.

2. **Cultivate Elite Inner Circles**

   - Establish tiered access: a public "outer court"
     where newcomers mingle, and an "inner chamber"
     for paying members, superfans, or trusted
     contributors. Offer exclusive AMAs,
     behind-the-scenes updates, and early content
     previews to your inner circle.

   - This mirrors the Renaissance practice of granting
     coveted court positions—chamberlain, privy
     councilor—to those most loyal, fostering a sense of
     honor and belonging.

3. **Empower Community Stewardship**

   - Recruit volunteer moderators and community
     champions. Provide them with style guides,
     moderation handbooks, and private channels
     where they can propose events, share feedback,
     and flag issues.

   - As Machiavelli notes, "the mercenary soldier is
     disloyal," but a citizen fighting for his hometown will
     defend it with zeal. Your moderators, invested in the
     community's well-being, become guardians against
     trolls and toxic drama.

4. **Design Rituals and Ceremonies**

- Regular events—weekly live chats, monthly challenges, or quarterly virtual conferences—forge collective identity. Celebrate milestones: the community's "anniversary," subscriber landmarks, or successful collaborative projects.

- Renaissance courts held elaborate festivals to remind subjects of the prince's grandeur; your digital ceremonies underscore shared values and reinforce bonds.

5. **Foster Peer-to-Peer Collaboration**

- Encourage members to form subgroups around smaller interests. Provide template channels—#project-showcase, #resource-exchange, #crit-circle—so that participants help one another grow.

- When subjects aid each other, the prince's burden lightens. Similarly, a self-sustaining community nurtures loyalty more effectively than top-down direction alone.

6. **Listen and Iterate**

- Deploy quarterly "council polls" and suggestion boxes. Share transparency reports: membership growth, event attendance, and feature roadmap status.

- o   Machiavelli praised rulers who adapted laws to popular custom; by evolving your community based on member feedback, you maintain relevance and prevent rebellion.

7. **Safeguard Against Factions**

   - o   Be vigilant for splinter groups or power blocs forming around individual influencers within your community. Distribute privileges evenly and rotate leadership roles to prevent any single voice from eclipsing the collective mission.

   - o   Just as a prince keeps noble houses in balance to avoid a coup, you manage sub-group dynamics to preserve unity.

By establishing a fortified community hub—complete with elite circles, active stewardship, shared rituals, and responsive governance—you translate Machiavelli's prescriptions for statecraft into digital relationship management.

Action Steps: Outreach Email Scripts; Partnership Scorecard

Outreach Email Scripts

1. **Initial Collaboration Inquiry**

   Subject: Exploring a Collaboration Opportunity

   Hi [Name],

   I've been following your work on [Platform/Topic] and was impressed by [Specific Detail]. I specialize in [Your Niche], and I believe a joint [Podcast Episode/Guest Post/Co-Stream] could bring valuable insights to both our audiences.

   Here's a rough proposal:

   1. Format: [e.g., 30-minute livestream Q&A]

   2. Proposed Date Range: [Two-week window]

   3. Mutual Promotion Plan: [Newsletter mention, social shares, cross-posting]

2. I'm happy to adjust details to suit your schedule and objectives. Would you be open to a brief call next week to explore this?

    Looking forward to the possibility of working together.

    Best,
    [Your Name] | [Your Channel/Brand] | [Contact Info]

3. **Follow-Up and Confirmation**

    Subject: Re: Collaboration Opportunity

    Hi [Name],

    Just circling back on my previous email regarding a potential [Collaboration Type]. I'd love to lock in details so we can plan promotion effectively.

    Does [Date/Time Option 1] or [Date/Time Option 2] work for a quick chat?

    Thanks again for considering—excited about what we can create together.

    Cheers,
    [Your Name]

4. **Thank-You and Next Steps**

Subject: Thank You + Next Steps for Our Collaboration

Hi [Name],

Thanks for the great conversation today! Here's what we agreed on:

1. [Deliverable A and Due Date]

2. [Deliverable B and Due Date]

3. Promotion Plan: [Details]

5. I'll draft a shared calendar invite and a brief agreement doc for both of us to sign. Please let me know if any adjustments are needed.

Looking forward to making this a success!

Best regards,
[Your Name]

Partnership Scorecard

Use these criteria to evaluate potential or ongoing collaborations. Rate each on a scale of 1–5, then calculate a total out of 25.

Partnerships scoring above 20 are high-value; those below 15 warrant renegotiation or cautious engagement.

- **Audience Alignment**: How closely does their demographic and psychographic profile match yours?

- **Engagement Quality**: Do their followers actively comment, share, and convert, or merely scroll past?

- **Production Standards**: Does their content meet professional quality in audio, video, or writing?

- **Reliability & Communication**: Have they met deadlines and responded promptly in past collaborations?

- **Growth Potential**: Will this partnership open doors to new markets, verticals, or monetization models?

After each joint project, revisit the scorecard. Celebrate high scorers with deeper integration; for lower scorers, discuss adjustments or explore alternative alliances.

By mastering strategic partnerships, practicing disciplined influencer diplomacy, and fostering a vibrant, well-guarded community hub, you build an interconnected network that elevates your influence and shields you from the isolation that dooms so many solo creators. In Machiavellian terms, you transform mercenary attachments into loyal auxiliaries, ensuring that your principality—the realm of your content—stands firm against the tides of change.

Chapter 4: The Art of Perception Management

Curating Your Persona: Authenticity vs. Aspiration

In *The Prince*, Machiavelli insists that a ruler's success depends less on his private virtues than on the image he projects: "It is not essential… that a prince should possess all the good qualities…I have enumerated, but it is very essential that he should seem to possess them." For the content creator, your persona—the living embodiment of your brand—must balance genuine self-expression with an aspirational ideal that inspires loyalty.

Begin by inventorying your core values, strengths, and passions. What drives you to create? Perhaps you're propelled by a desire to educate, to entertain, or to empower. Let these genuine motivations anchor your persona in authenticity. Yet recognize that raw authenticity without refinement can appear unfocused: a stream of consciousness that invites confusion rather than allegiance.

Next, define the aspirational dimension. Machiavelli advises princes to "appear merciful, faithful, humane, upright, and religious," even if they sometimes act otherwise. Your audience craves a hero they can root for—someone who embodies the transformation they themselves seek. If you teach productivity, your persona might project calm mastery over time, hinting at the peace your methods promise. If you create wellness content, you might emphasize serene confidence, even as you share your own struggles behind the scenes.

Weave authenticity and aspiration into a coherent brand narrative. Share candid anecdotes—early failures, personal doubts, behind-the-lens moments—to establish trust. Then layer in the aspirational vision: the image of competence, clarity, or creativity that you're guiding your followers toward. Position yourself as a living case study: "Here's where I was, and here's where the system I've developed can take you."

Consistency is key. A Machiavellian prince who oscillates between generosity and cruelty confuses his subjects; likewise, if your persona swings between self-deprecating vulnerability one day and über-expert confidence the next, your community may feel unmoored. Create a persona matrix: list your core traits (e.g., "approachable expert," "creative disruptor," "strategic mentor") and audit each piece of content against it. Does this livestream moment reinforce your ideal, or does it undercut it?

Finally, refine over time. Machiavelli's prince never stops calculating the effect of his actions on public perception. Solicit feedback through polls and one-on-one conversations. When audience members describe you in their own words ("I see you as a trusted coach" or "You're that friend who keeps me honest"), you gain invaluable data on which aspects of your persona truly resonate—and which you may need to dial back or amplify.

Visual Consistency: Thumbnails, Color Palettes, and Logos

"A prince ought to have no other aim… but war and its organization and discipline," Machiavelli writes, underscoring the necessity of methodical, disciplined presentation. In the visual realm, discipline manifests as consistency: a unified visual identity that tells viewers at a glance, "This is yours."

Start with thumbnails—the storefront of each video or post. Choose a consistent layout: a bold headline font, your face or a signature icon in the same position, and a background treatment that echoes your color palette. Over time, regular viewers will scroll past dozens of items before sensing, almost subconsciously, "Ah, here's [Your Name]."

Select a palette of two or three primary colors and two neutrals. Machiavelli's courts often used heraldic colors to signal allegiance; your palette signals your brand family. Do these colors evoke the mood and values you stand for—energizing oranges for creativity, calming teals for mindfulness, or authoritative navy for business expertise? Apply them across your website, social banners, presentation slides, and post graphics.

Your logo functions like a coat of arms. It should be simple enough to scale from a 16×16 favicon to a 1080×1080 social avatar, yet distinctive. If you choose a monogram of your initials, integrate a subtle symbol that ties into your niche—an open book for educators, a microphone for podcasters, or a compass for explorers of new ideas. Once designed, treat it as sacred: guard against unapproved variants or off-brand color shifts.

Document these visual rules in a living Brand Style Guide. Include specifications for safe margin sizes around your logo, font choices with hierarchy (headline, subhead, body text), and do's and don'ts ("Never stretch the logo," "Always use grayscale filter on lifestyle photos before overlaying text"). Machiavelli's ideal prince would have left no ambiguity about court protocol—neither should you about your visual protocol.

Finally, audit visually every quarter. Just as a prince inspects his fortress walls, inspect your feed, your channel homepage, and your newsletter template. Replace stray images or outdated banners. Weed out any rogue posts that violate your guide. This disciplined maintenance ensures that new followers always encounter a cohesive world—one where every element reinforces your authority and identity.

Storytelling as Spin: Positioning Your Narrative

Machiavelli wrote that history favors the prince "who can make a legend of himself or the memory of his state." Your content narrative must similarly weave individual posts into an overarching legend—one that positions you as both guide and protagonist in a shared journey with your audience.

Identify the central conflict or transformation at the heart of your work. Is it "Overcoming the overwhelm of modern life"? Is it "Building a business from zero to six figures"? Frame each piece of content as a chapter in that larger story. Introduce challenges (the dragons), showcase lessons (the cunning tactics), and celebrate wins (the triumphant reveal).

Use the classic three-act structure. **Act I** sets the stage: introduce the problem or context. **Act II** deepens the stakes: reveal obstacles, false starts, or market shifts. **Act III** delivers resolution: actionable takeaways, proofs of concept, or calls to adventure for your audience. Machiavelli's own writings often present historical case studies—like Cesare Borgia's cunning maneuvers—as narrative vignettes. Likewise, sprinkle your content with real-world examples: your own experiments, your audience's successes, or industry anecdotes.

Adopt strategic "spin" techniques. Highlight your wins but own your missteps. When you share a failed launch, frame it as a laboratory result that informed your subsequent success. Use metaphors and analogies that resonate with your niche: a marketing funnel becomes a castle moat protecting resources; a launch calendar becomes a campaign plan to siege an industry stronghold.

Anchor every narrative with clear positioning statements. Begin videos with "Here's how most creators get stuck… and here's the three-step strategy I used to break free." Conclude with "If you want to join me on this path, here's your next mission." Machiavelli knew a prince must give subjects a sense of purpose; your call-to-action is that purpose for your community.

Finally, maintain narrative coherence across platforms. If your YouTube series introduces your origin story, have your newsletter sequence pick up with deeper background, and let your Instagram Stories offer "director's cut" insights. Machiavelli's court artisans produced tapestries, frescoes, and poems all reinforcing the same royal myth—your cross-channel storytelling should similarly erect a unified mythos around your brand.

Action Steps: Brand Style Guide; Narrative Storyboard

1. Craft Your Brand Style Guide

- **Logo & Variations**: Finalize your primary logo, icon-only mark, and any lockups with wordmarks.

- **Color Palette**: Define HEX/RGB codes for your two primaries, two secondaries, and two neutrals.

- **Typography**: Select one display font for headlines, one serif or sans-serif for body copy, and any accent fonts.

- **Imagery Guidelines**: Outline photo treatments—filters, overlays, framing—and iconography style (line weight, corner radius).

- **Layout Rules**: Specify grid margins, whitespace requirements, and recommended thumbnail composition.

- **Usage Examples**: Show a correct and an incorrect implementation for each major element.

Store this guide in a shared folder and reference it whenever creating batch assets. Review quarterly and update whenever you evolve your visual persona.

2. Develop a Narrative Storyboard

- **Core Arc Definition**: In a single paragraph, describe your "hero's journey" framework—your audience's transformation from Point A to Point B.

- **Chapter Outlines**: Break the journey into five to seven thematic beats (e.g., "Awakening," "Trial by Fire," "Discovery," "Mastery").

- **Content Mapping**: For each beat, list two to three content ideas—blogs, videos, podcasts—that illustrate it. Note format, title hook, and key takeaways.

- **Emotional Touchpoints**: Annotate where to evoke vulnerability, triumph, humor, or curiosity.

- **Cross-Platform Beats**: Indicate which beats get depth in long-form (YouTube or podcast) and which get quick reinforcement in short-form (social stories, tweets).

- **Milestone Calls-to-Action**: Assign CTAs—newsletter signup, course registration, community invite—to pivotal story moments.

With this storyboard, you'll never post ad hoc again. Each piece of content becomes an intentional narrative step, advancing the shared journey and deepening your audience's investment.

By mastering the art of perception management—curating a persona that harmonizes authenticity and aspiration, enforcing visual consistency, and wielding storytelling as strategic spin—you craft not just content, but a commanding presence. Like Machiavelli's ideal prince, you shape not only the substance of your rule but the very way your subjects perceive it, ensuring that your influence endures beyond any single post or platform.

Chapter 5: Reputation and Credibility

Machiavellian Reputation Tactics: Praise, Blame, and Selective Disclosure

Reputation is the lifeblood of rulership; without it, a prince's every word is met with suspicion, and his every order with caution. Niccolò Machiavelli opens *The Prince* by emphasizing that "the vulgar crowd always is taken by appearances, and by the outcome of things rather than by the causes which produce them." In other words, people judge more on what they see and hear than on the underlying reality. For the content creator, this translates into the imperative to shape perception through carefully orchestrated reputation tactics: deploying praise to highlight allies, directing blame to neutralize detractors, and releasing just enough information to maintain authority without overexposure.

Praise as Public Currency
Praise in a digital context functions like the distribution of titles and honors in a Renaissance court. Machiavelli notes that a wise prince knows how to reward those whose talents and loyalty serve his realm, for "gifts properly bestowed make one loved by all." In practice, content creators use praise to spotlight community members, collaborators, and even competitors when appropriate. By publicly acknowledging constructive feedback—"Shout-out to @jane_doe for suggesting our latest topic, which sparked 500

comments!"—you confer social capital on your allies. This not only strengthens their loyalty, but also signals to onlookers that you are generous, attentive, and confident enough to share the spotlight.

However, praise must be strategic and selective. Over-praising trivial contributions dilutes its value; under-praising key supporters breeds resentment. Maintain a ledger—an informal mental tally—of those who consistently add value: guest contributors who deliver polished write-ups, beta-testers who catch critical bugs, or superfans who drive meaningful discussions. When the time is right—after a major course launch, a high-stakes livestream, or a viral post—award these champions with elevated roles (early access, custom badges, exclusive interviews). This mirrors Machiavelli's practice of elevating deserving courtiers to positions of influence, ensuring that your domain thrives on a foundation of mutual respect and reciprocal loyalty.

Blame as Boundary Setting

 Just as praise reinforces bonds, blame delineates boundaries. In Machiavelli's view, a prince must never shy away from castigating those who threaten his authority: "It is a dangerous thing to rely upon the public's good will." When a member of your community violates core values—spreads misinformation, harasses other users, or undermines your brand's integrity—swift and visible corrective action is essential. Public reprimands, temporary suspensions, or removal of privileges serve two purposes: they demonstrate to the broader audience that you uphold standards, and they discourage future transgressions.

Yet, as Machiavelli warns, excessive severity can provoke fear and resentment: "Men offend sooner in the cause of love than in the cause of fear." The key is calibrated response. Draft clear community guidelines that codify acceptable behavior and specify consequences. When violations occur, reference these guidelines explicitly: "As per our community charter, posts containing hate speech will be removed, and repeat offenders will be banned for 30 days." Such transparency defuses claims of arbitrary punishment. After the sanction is served, consider a path to redemption—allow offenders to appeal or demonstrate reformed conduct—so that your realm remains just rather than purely punitive.

Selective Disclosure for Strategic Ambiguity
 Machiavelli famously counsels, "A prince ought to inspire fear in such a way that, if he does not win love, he avoids hatred." Part of inspiring disciplined respect lies in the art of what he calls "appropriate secrecy": revealing enough to maintain trust, yet withholding details that could embolden adversaries. For a creator, selective disclosure means sharing genuine progress updates and behind-the-scenes glimpses, while keeping sensitive business intelligence—like partnership negotiations, algorithm insights, or unpublished monetization strategies—confined to trusted circles.

Implement this by tiering information release across public posts, subscriber-only newsletters, and private mastermind groups. Publicly, share the success story: "We've crossed 50,000 subscribers and are thrilled with your support!" In a subscriber-only update, reveal interim metrics, challenges encountered, and experimental pivots. In your private community, discuss detailed launch data, revenue splits, and upcoming collaboration opportunities. This three-tier approach mirrors a prince's use of public proclamations, confidential counsel to nobles, and secret strategy sessions with the inner circle. By controlling the flow of information, you maintain an aura of competence and progress, while safeguarding the specifics that might advantage competitors or alarm less invested followers.

Through a disciplined regimen of praise to reinforce loyalty, measured blame to uphold standards, and selective disclosure to preserve strategic advantage, you cultivate a reputation that commands respect. Your audience comes to see you not only as a source of value, but as a leader whose authority rests on thoughtful governance.

Social Proof: Testimonials, Reviews, and User-Generated Content

Machiavelli observes that "men more quickly forget the death of their father than the loss of their patrimony"—people remember tangible, material benefits more than abstract sentiment. In the realm of digital influence, social proof serves as that tangible patrimony: visible endorsements, success stories, and content created by fans validate your authority and entice newcomers to join your fold.

Testimonials as Shining Endorsements
 Collect and display testimonials from satisfied customers, collaborators, or community leaders. Solicit short, punchy statements that highlight specific outcomes: "After following [Your Course], I doubled my email list in just four weeks," or "Working with [Your Name] transformed my approach to storytelling." Position these endorsements prominently on sales pages, video landing screens, and in your newsletter header. In Machiavellian

terms, each testimonial functions like a noble's seal of approval, certifying to all that your methods yield concrete results.

To ensure authenticity, gather testimonials through structured prompts—ask users what skeptical thoughts they had before trying your content, which exact module or tip made the biggest difference, and what measurable progress they achieved. Then, edit for clarity but preserve the original voice. Consider recording short video testimonials; seeing a real person speak to your impact is more persuasive than text alone. Like a prince parading his trophies in the public square, showcase these narratives to bolster your claim to expertise.

Reviews as Real-Time Market Feedback
 Reviews—star ratings, comments on platforms, feedback threads—serve a dual purpose: they guide potential subscribers' decisions and give you timely insights into areas for improvement. Encourage customers to leave reviews by sending post-purchase emails with a direct link to your preferred review platform. Offer an incentive—such as entry into a giveaway or a small resource download—in exchange for a candid review. The influx of fresh reviews signals vibrancy and community engagement, reassuring prospects that your offerings are relevant and valued.

Monitor review sentiment through a simple dashboard or notifications. Machiavelli warns that princes must be "ever mindful of the common people's whispers." Negative reviews, while uncomfortable, often contain kernels of truth—unclear instructions, buggy resources, or unfulfilled promises. Analyze recurring themes, address them in your next release, and publicly note the changes you've made. For example: "Thank you to reviewers who pointed out that Module 3 lacked a walkthrough—this week we added a 20-minute demo that clarifies each step." This responsiveness not only improves your product but also demonstrates that you value user input and act on it.

User-Generated Content as Proof of Enthusiasm
 Nothing speaks louder than fans producing content on your behalf. Reposts of your key visuals, fan-made tutorials, challenges, or case-study videos extend your reach while implicitly testifying to your value. To encourage this, launch branded hashtags—"#30DayGrowthChallenge"—and prompt followers to document their daily wins. Host contests that reward the most creative or helpful user submissions, and then elevate the winners on your channels.

Share UGC (user-generated content) in your own feed with captions like, "Check out how @alex_design applied our branding template to launch her new shop!" These reshared moments not only validate your frameworks but also foster a sense of belonging among participants. Machiavelli might have equated this to the way a prince would commission artworks celebrating his victories—each mural or tapestry broadcasting his prowess. Your digital gallery of UGC similarly broadcasts your influencer prowess across platforms.

By orchestrating testimonials, galvanizing reviews, and amplifying user-generated content, you create a self-reinforcing ecosystem of social proof. Every newcomer who sees a stream of authentic voices singing your praises encounters an irresistible invitation to join the ranks.

Handling Crisis: Apology vs. Pivot Strategies

Even the most skillful prince faces crises—failed sieges, treacherous betrayals, or unexpected rebellions. Machiavelli devotes an entire chapter to "the dangers of taking counsel only from friends," advising that one must plan for worst-case scenarios. For a content creator, crises come in many forms: a major technical glitch during a live launch, accusations of plagiarism, a public gaffe, or an algorithmic penalty that slashes reach. Your response determines whether the setback becomes a ruin or a rallying point.

When to Apologize: Owning the Error
 An apology is appropriate when the fault lies clearly with you—misleading claims, offensive language, broken promises, or undisclosed sponsorships. Machiavelli insists that "it is necessary for a prince to know well how to feign goodness, and to be a great pretender and dissembler." However, in the age of transparency, feigning goodness without genuine contrition backfires spectacularly. A timely, sincere apology diffuses anger and rebuilds trust.

Craft your apology by addressing four key elements:

1. **Acknowledgment**: State plainly what went wrong—"I failed to proofread our latest newsletter, resulting in incorrect data."

2. **Responsibility**: Use "I" language—"I take full responsibility for this oversight."

3. **Correction**: Explain what you've done to fix the issue—"We've corrected the data and sent updated information to all subscribers."

4. **Reassurance**: Detail steps to prevent recurrence—"Going forward, we've implemented a two-step review process for all send-outs."

Issue this apology publicly on the same channels where the harm occurred. Machiavelli would have his prince stand before the people, not hide from them; likewise, your willingness to be visible in remediation enhances credibility.

When to Pivot: Redirecting the Narrative
 Not every crisis stems from clear fault. Sometimes external forces—industry shifts, platform policy changes, or market disruptions—necessitate a rapid strategic pivot. In these cases, a full apology can seem weak or irrelevant. Instead, adopt what we'll call a "pivot strategy": acknowledge the new reality, present a revised vision, and frame it as an evolution rather than an admission of failure.

For instance, if a core feature of your course is suddenly deprecated by a software update, announce: "Due to recent changes in [Platform], our curriculum will adapt to current tools. We're excited to introduce alternative workflows in Modules 4 and 5 that not only match but exceed the previous capabilities." Here, you neither apologize for circumstances beyond your control nor ignore the audience's need for guidance. You pivot, demonstrating agility and forward-thinking.

Machiavelli admired leaders who could turn adversity into opportunity, praising those who "know how to profit from the times." By reframing setbacks as the impetus for innovation—teasing new features, hosting brainstorming livestreams, or soliciting community input for the next iteration—you transform the crisis into a collaborative growth moment.

Blending Apology and Pivot
 Certain crises demand a hybrid approach. Suppose you inadvertently share unverified statistics in a keynote, sparking claims of misinformation. Begin with apology—acknowledge the slip and correct the record—then pivot to a deeper commitment: "Moving forward, we'll integrate real-time data dashboards and regular fact-checks into our presentations. I invite you to join our upcoming roundtable on data integrity so we can co-develop best practices."

This dual approach satisfies the audience's call for accountability while channeling their energy into constructive next steps. Machiavelli's ideal prince would accept responsibility for a failed tax policy, then rally his citizens with a new prosperity plan. You too can convert crisis-born mistrust into renewed engagement.

Action Steps: Reputation Tracker; Crisis Response Flowchart

Reputation Tracker

1. **Metrics Dashboard**

   - List key reputation indicators: positive mentions, negative mentions, average sentiment score, number of testimonials, and volume of user-generated content.

   - Use social-listening tools or manual weekly reviews to log these numbers in a simple spreadsheet.

2. **Qualitative Journal**

   - Record notable praise, constructive critiques, and crisis flares (e.g., "05/12: User X called out error in pricing; responded with correction and apology.").

   - Note your response time, channels used, and outcome (e.g., "Issue resolved within 24 hours; follow-up post reached 1,200 views.").

3. **Monthly Review**

   - Analyze trends: Are positive mentions increasing? Is sentiment improving? Is UGC growing?

- o Flag patterns requiring action—consistent feedback themes, recurring technical issues, or unexplained sentiment dips.

4. **Reputation Score**

   - o Assign weights to each indicator (e.g., testimonials 30%, sentiment 25%, UGC 20%, mention volume 15%, crisis resolution speed 10%).

   - o Calculate a composite score to track over time, aiming for gradual quarterly improvement.

Crisis Response Flowchart

1. **Detection**

   - o Input: Alert from monitoring tool, user DM, or comment flag.

2. **Triage**

   - o Severity assessment: Low (minor typo), Medium (misleading info or user complaint), High (offensive content or data breach).

3. **Decision Node**

   - o If Low → Edit quietly or note for next update.

- ○ If Medium → Issue public clarification or apology.

- ○ If High → Initiate full crisis protocol.

4. **Action Branches**

   - ○ **Public Apology**: Draft statement with acknowledgment, responsibility, correction, reassurance. Publish on all affected channels.

   - ○ **Pivot Announcement**: Outline external change, revised plan, next-step invitation.

   - ○ **Combined**: Layer apology into pivot message.

5. **Follow-Up**

   - ○ Send detailed update via email or private community.

   - ○ Host live Q&A or town-hall livestream within 48 hours.

6. **Post-Mortem**

   - ○ Convene a short internal review: What went wrong? How effective was the response? What gaps remain?

   - ○ Update guidelines and flowchart based on lessons learned.

By systematically tracking your reputation and equipping yourself with a structured crisis response, you ensure that no setback goes unaddressed and no achievement uncelebrated. In doing so, you build a fortress of credibility that withstands the storms of digital fame—just as Machiavelli's ideal prince secures his principality through vigilant governance and adaptive resilience.

Chapter 6: The Power of Surprise and Innovation

Throughout *The Prince*, Machiavelli reminds us that stagnation is death and that true greatness belongs to those who innovate boldly. He declares, "Whosoever desires constant success must change his conduct with the times," urging rulers to embrace disruption rather than cling to convention. For content creators navigating ever-shifting platforms and fickle algorithms, surprise and innovation aren't luxuries—they're lifelines. In this chapter, we'll explore how viral pivots rewrite the rules, how to sense the right moment for bold experiments, how to balance the new with the familiar, and how to systematize these practices through innovation sprints and testing matrices.

Disruption over Convention: Case Studies of Viral Pivots

Machiavelli warns that established methods can become traps: "Princedoms accustomed to their own laws… are less difficult to hold than new ones, but new ordinances are always dangerous." In content terms, what once worked—long-form essays, flat thumbnails, predictable series—can suddenly fail to capture attention. The antidote? A well-timed, well-executed pivot that surprises audiences, leverages momentum, and repositions your brand at the forefront of innovation.

Case Study 1: From Lecture Halls to Sketch Comedy

Consider Dr. Emma Caldwell, a university lecturer who built a modest following through hour-long recorded seminars on ancient philosophy. After noticing her students' waning engagement—even as downloads ticked upward—she experimented with 60-second comedic sketches that distilled core ideas into absurdist skits. Overnight, her channel exploded: what had been niche academic fare transformed into shareable comedy that introduced new viewers to classical thought.

- **The Pivot**: Shifting from length and rigor to brevity and humor.

- **The Surprise Element**: Philosophy delivered as slapstick, complete with toga-clad actors and puns.

- **Outcome**: A tenfold increase in subscribers within two weeks, broader media coverage, and invitations to mainstream podcasts.

This aligns with Machiavelli's directive that "a prince must sometimes adopt measures which, though unpleasant to grant, are indispensable to preserve his state." Emma's shift was uncomfortable—she risked alienating her original base—but the resulting growth secured her influence far more solidly than academic prestige alone.

Case Study 2: The Silent Vlog Experiment

In mid-2023, tech reviewer Leo Morales noticed his view counts plateauing despite steady upload schedules. Machiavelli teaches that "men change their ruler… when they find themselves oppressed," and Leo felt burdened by expectations of in-depth gadget teardowns. In response, he released a surprise "silent vlog"—a cinematic, music-driven 5-minute montage of him exploring a bustling city, gadget-free.

- **The Pivot**: Stepping away from reviews to showcase real-world living, sans commentary.

- **The Surprise Element**: Subverting a tech channel's formula by delivering pure visuals and ambient sound.

- **Outcome**: The video went viral across lifestyle and travel communities, drawing new subscribers who then discovered his tech content.

By adopting this unorthodox format, Leo embodied Machiavelli's principle that "innovation owes its success to the fact that… it delights." The silent vlog delighted viewers precisely because it defied category expectations.

Case Study 3: Live-Streamed Choose-Your-Own-Adventure

Gaming streamer Alicia "Alix" Tran enjoyed a loyal but modest following for her playthroughs. Inspired by the interactive epics of tabletop RPGs, and recalling Machiavelli's praise of audacity—"Fortune favors the bold"—she announced a live series where viewers voted in real time on every decision her character made.

- **The Pivot**: Introducing communal decision-making to a typically solo playstyle.

- **The Surprise Element**: Real-time polls that shaped narrative twists, from alliances to betrayals.

- **Outcome**: Concurrent viewership soared, chat engagement skyrocketed, and sponsorships for interactive gaming tools followed.

Alix's experiment underscores that surprise need not be grandiose; it can be as simple as handing creative control to your audience and trusting the chaos to produce novel, shareable moments.

Timing and Rhythm: When to Launch Bold Experiments

Machiavelli counsels, "He who is highly esteemed is not easily conspired against," but he also warns that "one change always leaves open a road to others." In content creation, timing a pivot poorly can erode your credibility; timing it well can position you as a visionary.

Reading the Signals

1. **Plateaus and Declines**

   - Drops in watch time, subscriber growth, or engagement often signal the need for innovation. Machiavelli believed that "everyone sees what you appear to be, few experience what you really are." If analytics reveal stasis, you must reveal a new facet of your brand to stay compelling.

2. **Platform Shifts**

   - Algorithm updates, feature rollouts (like a new Stories format), or emerging network trends create windows of opportunity. As Machiavelli says, "Nothing is more difficult than… to introduce a new order of things." Yet these windows, though narrow, let you position yourself as an early adopter.

3. **Cultural Moments**

   - Viral challenges, seasonal events, or global conversations can serve as natural jump-off points. A beauty creator who launches a skincare series tied to World Wellness Day, or a finance influencer who debuts budgeting tips at tax-season peaks, harnesses external momentum for internal innovation.

Establishing Your Experimental Cadence

- **Monthly Micro-Experiments**
  Dedicate one piece of content per month to a low-risk test—a new thumbnail style, a different intro length, a guest host cameo. Track performance against baseline metrics. Machiavelli prized small-scale incursions into enemy territory before full invasions; think of micro-experiments as reconnaissance missions.

- **Quarterly Macro-Pivots**
  Every three months, plan a larger experiment—a format overhaul, a cross-platform launch, or a major live event. Buffer these with planning sprints and postmortem sessions. Machiavelli noted that "fortune is a woman, and… to master her is to beat her into submission by violence," meaning that decisive, forceful action often yields the greatest returns.

- **Seasonal Reviews**
  Align experiments with seasonal cycles—holidays, academic semesters, fiscal quarters—so that your innovations resonate with audience mindsets. A productivity channel might debut a "Back-to-School Bootcamp" in August; a wellness influencer might trial a "New Year, New You" challenge in December.

Synchronizing with Audience Rhythm

Know when your audience is most receptive to novelty. If your core viewers expect consistency on Mondays and Thursdays, avoid launching radical formats then. Instead, use a mid-week slot—Wednesday surprise streams or Saturday deep-dives—so your existing audience has space to acclimate before your signature content returns. Machiavelli would argue for preserving the rituals that build trust while interweaving fresh elements at strategic intervals.

Balancing "Fresh" with "Familiar": A/B Testing for Creatives

"A prudent prince ought to examine everything, and… show himself adaptable." In content, adaptability hinges on your ability to balance the new with the known. Too much novelty alienates; too much routine bores. A/B testing provides the scientific precision to calibrate this balance.

Designing Your Tests

1. **Define Clear Variables**

   - Thumbnails: color scheme A vs. B

   - Titles: benefit-driven headline vs. curiosity-driven headline

   - Intros: personal anecdote vs. data point

- ○ Calls to Action: "Subscribe now" button vs. "Join the community" link

2. **Segment Audience Fairly**

   - ○ Deploy variants to statistically similar audience slices. Platforms like YouTube Premiere A/B testing or email subject-line split tests ensure you're comparing apples to apples.

3. **Measure Impact Across Metrics**

   - ○ Click-through rate (CTR) for thumbnails

   - ○ View duration and watch time for intros

   - ○ Engagement rate for CTAs

   - ○ Conversion rate for download or sign-up links

Interpreting Results

- **Statistical Significance**
  Avoid overreacting to minor CTR fluctuations. Machiavelli valued measured judgment: "One change always leaves open a road to others." Only adopt changes when confidence intervals exceed your thresholds—say, 95% confidence—to prevent oscillating between fads.

- **Contextual Insights**
  'A thumbnail that performs better on a Tuesday might falter

on a weekend. Always consider timing and content type context. Document patterns over multiple cycles before cementing the change into your brand style guide.

Iterative Refinement

View A/B tests as continuous dialogue with your audience. Machiavelli reminds us that "fortune… varies, and cannot always be counted on." What works today may falter tomorrow. Build A/B testing into your content calendar so that it becomes a perpetual engine of incremental innovation.

Action Steps: Innovation Sprint Plan; Testing Matrix

To transform these principles into practice, adopt a structured approach that mirrors agile methodologies, with sprints, backlogs, and clear success metrics.

1. Innovation Sprint Plan

- **Sprint Length**: 2–4 weeks

- **Sprint Goals**: Define one major pivot theme (e.g., "Humor infusion," "Interactive elements," "Minimalist visuals").

- **Backlog Creation**: Brainstorm 8–10 experiment ideas aligned with the theme. Prioritize by expected impact and feasibility.

- **Sprint Kickoff**: Convene a planning session—solo or with your team—to assign responsibilities, set deadlines, and establish measurement frameworks.

- **Execution Phase**: Develop, deploy, and monitor each experiment. Use project-management tools to track progress and flag blockers.

- **Review & Retrospective**: At sprint's end, analyze performance data, document learnings, and decide which experiments to scale, iterate, or retire. Update your content calendar with the next sprint's theme.

2. Testing Matrix

Maintain an accessible, living document—whether in a shared doc, a project-management board, or even a physical whiteboard—where each experiment is tracked using these four dimensions:

- **Experiment Type:** Clearly label what aspect you're testing (for example, thumbnail style, title format, intro length, CTA wording, or overall format variation).

- **Variable A vs. Variable B:**

  - For **Thumbnail Style**, compare "bold text overlay" against "face-only portrait."

- For **Title Format**, pit a "benefit highlight" headline against a "curiosity hook."

- For **Intro Length**, test a 5-second opener versus a 15-second one.

- For **CTA Wording**, try "Subscribe now" against "Join our tribe."

- For **Format Variation**, experiment with a solo vlog format versus a guest-interview style.

- **Primary Metric:** Decide in advance which performance indicator you'll use to judge the test—click-through rate for thumbnails, a combination of CTR and average watch time for titles, 30-second retention for intros, conversion rate for CTAs, and overall engagement rate (comments, shares) for format experiments.

- **Winner Criteria:** Establish your threshold for success before launching:

  - Thumbnails should deliver at least a 10% uplift in CTR over your baseline.

  - Titles must improve CTR by 5% and boost average watch time by 10%.

  - Intros should raise 30-second retention by 8%.

  - CTAs need a minimum 3% lift in conversions.

- Format variations aim for a 15% increase in comments.

Implementation Tips:

- Keep this experiment log where your whole team can see it and contribute.

- Update the results every week, noting which variable won and by how much.

- Annotate unexpected insights—such as, "The curiosity-hook title outperformed the benefit headline by 20% among viewers aged 18–24"—so you capture audience nuances that might inform future tests.

By embracing disruption over stale convention, mastering the timing and rhythm of bold experiments, and rigorously balancing the new with the familiar through A/B testing, you harness Machiavelli's timeless wisdom to forge a content strategy that outpaces rivals. With a formalized innovation sprint plan and a dynamic testing matrix, surprise becomes not a one-off stunt but the engine of continuous evolution—ensuring that, like the most successful princes of history, your realm of content thrives in any age.

Chapter 7: Competitive Analysis

Mapping Rival Creators: Strengths, Weaknesses, and Openings

In *The Prince*, Machiavelli insists that a successful ruler must "have no other aim or thought, nor take up any other thing for his study, but war and its organization and discipline." In the realm of content creation, "war" is the battle for attention, authority, and influence. To prevail, you must know your competitors as well as you know your audience. Only by dissecting their strengths, weaknesses, and the gaps they leave open can you chart a decisive path to dominance.

Identifying Your Principal Rivals

Begin by listing the creators who vie directly for your niche's spotlight. If you produce long-form investigative podcasts, identify the top five channels that consistently attract your ideal listener. If your forte is short lifestyle reels, note the three or four influencers whose styling, music choices, or cadence most closely mirror—or outshine—your own. Refer back to Machiavelli's counsel that "a prince ought to rely on himself and not on others." While you'll learn from rivals, you must craft your own strategy rather than merely mimic theirs.

Cataloguing Strengths

For each rival, catalog their core competencies. Does one boast cinematic production values that captivate viewers? Another may excel at rapid-fire community engagement, replying to comments within minutes and forging personal bonds. Perhaps a third has a knack for securing high-profile guests or brand partnerships that lend credibility by association. Record these strengths in vivid detail: the exact editing techniques that set a rival's thumbnails ablaze, the cadence and linguistic hooks in their hooks that yield click-through rates of 20%, or the ingenious ways they "gamify" tutorials to sustain binge-watch sessions.

Machiavelli admired princes who understood their own—and their enemies'—capabilities: "If an enterprise is difficult, men will more readily attempt it if it seems possible to achieve by their own exertions;" likewise, you must know whether a rival's prowess stems from deep expertise you can only approximate, or from surface-level tricks you can outmaneuver.

Exposing Weaknesses

But every competitor has chinks in the armor. Perhaps a top-ranking blogger relies on outdated SEO tactics that flounder on new algorithms. Maybe an otherwise polished YouTuber falters under live pressure, with awkward pauses and technical hiccups. A social-media star might generate flashy stories but lack substantive follow-through—posts that dazzle for a moment but provide little lasting value.

Machiavelli warns that "an enterprise which is other than good ought not to be attempted," suggesting that endeavors lacking solid foundations are doomed. Identify where each rival's foundation crumbles. Does their content leak credibility under scrutiny? Are they tethered to a single platform, vulnerable to policy changes? Do they neglect an entire sub-demographic, such as non-native-English speakers or older professionals? Chart these weaknesses precisely, for they are your points of entry.

Spotting Strategic Openings

With strengths and weaknesses mapped, seek openings—those gaps in the competitive terrain that you can inhabit. If no one offers bilingual commentary in your field, or if every major podcaster overlooks the intersection of your niche with mental-health insights, you have uncovered an opening. Machiavelli extols those who seize unguarded fortresses: "Fortune favors the daring." Threats to rival strongholds—shifting audience tastes, unaddressed subtopics, neglected formats—are invitations to stake your claim.

Begin sketching your competitor map as a mental grid: rivals arrayed along axes of "production polish" vs. "authentic relatability," "niche depth" vs. "broad topical appeal," or "community engagement" vs. "one-to-many broadcast." Position each competitor accordingly. The quadrants that remain sparse—perhaps "high polish, hyper-niche" or "deep academic rigor with daily community check-ins"—signal blue-ocean opportunities where you can flourish without head-on collision.

SWOT for Content Strategies

Machiavelli counsels that a shrewd prince must "look at the causes of things" to anticipate dangers and exploit advantages. A SWOT analysis—assessing Strengths, Weaknesses, Opportunities, and Threats—offers a structured lens for this examination. By applying SWOT to your content strategy, you transform vague hunches into concrete insights.

Strengths

Reflect on your unique assets. Do you possess a rare blend of technical expertise and storytelling charisma? Perhaps you have direct industry experience—ten years as a startup founder—while most competitors only curate second-hand insights. Your production team might include a graphic designer who crafts custom animations that no one else can replicate. List these strengths exhaustively, and then ask: how can I amplify them further? Machiavelli's ideal prince "who becomes great through his own arms" succeeds because he builds on intrinsic capabilities.

Weaknesses

Honesty is critical here. What do you lack? Is your equipment producing subpar audio? Do you struggle to meet your self-imposed publishing schedule? Perhaps your SEO knowledge is shallow, or your editing workflow leaves you no time for promotional activities. A prince who ignores his own lack of fortifications invites invasion; similarly, unaddressed weaknesses leave you open to competitive assault. Acknowledge them without judgment—only clear sight of your vulnerabilities permits targeted remediation.

Opportunities

This quadrant overlaps with the openings identified earlier, but it also considers external factors: emerging platforms (like a nascent short-form video app), cultural shifts (a new appetite for eco-conscious content), or technological innovations (interactive livestream extensions). Machiavelli admonishes princes to "take advantage of occasions," for fortune smiles on those who act quickly. Catalog these opportunities in detail: which upcoming conferences could you speak at? Are there trending keywords with low competition? Is there a partnership available that could introduce you to a fresh audience segment?

Threats

Finally, map threats—both direct and indirect. A rival's upcoming collaboration with a major sponsor might eclipse your own reach. Algorithm changes could de-prioritize your core format. Broader economic downturns may shrink advertising budgets and dry up sponsorships. Even shifts in audience behavior, like a migration from long-form consumption to bite-sized audio, pose threats. Machiavelli reminds princes that "new dangers arise when men think that all is secure," so you must anticipate and plan defensive measures: diversify revenue streams, build community-owned channels, and cultivate readiness to pivot formats.

By completing a rigorous SWOT, you emerge not only with a realistic self-portrait but with a prioritized action plan: double down on strengths, shore up weaknesses, seize top-ranked opportunities, and neutralize the gravest threats.

Blue-Ocean Content: Finding Uncontested Niches

Machiavelli knew that a wise prince should seek to govern lands unclaimed by others, rather than contest heavily fortified domains: "Whoever wants to obtain a state must either know how to attack it when it is naked and not fortified, or make it so." In content strategy, a "blue ocean" represents an uncontested niche where you can design value propositions that competitors haven't imagined.

Recognizing Red vs. Blue Oceans

A red ocean is a saturated field where many creators fight over the same audience segments with similar formats and messaging. Think "daily vlogs about productivity hacks" or "podcasts interviewing startup founders." In these arenas, war is bloody and margins thin. A blue ocean, by contrast, emerges when you identify unmet needs or reimagine existing topics through fresh lenses. For example, instead of general productivity hacks, you might target "neurodivergent entrepreneurs who need tailored time-management systems."

Systematic Blue-Ocean Discovery

1. **Audience Pain Points Beyond the Obvious**

   - Host candid conversations with your most engaged followers. Ask not only "What do you like?" but "What do you *really* need that you can't find anywhere?" The most valuable answers often lie in whispered frustrations—obstacles that mainstream creators overlook because they don't experience them personally.

2. **Cross-Industry Analogies**

   - Machiavelli prized generals who borrowed tactics from unexpected quarters. A digital-art creator might study print-magazine editorial calendars for content pacing; a fitness coach could adapt narrative hooks from genre-fiction authors. Identify practices outside your vertical, then experiment with transplanting them into your niche.

3. **Emerging Technologies and Formats**

   - Keep a watchful eye on platform betas, augmented-reality filters, or AI-powered editing tools. Early adopters of novel mediums—like 3D interactive tutorials—can capture audiences before competitors marshal their resources.

4. **Unserved or Underserved Segments**

   - Examine the demographics and psychographics of your field. Certain age groups, linguistic communities, or lifestyle cohorts may lack dedicated content creators. By designing offerings that speak their language—literally or figuratively—you cultivate a near-monopoly.

Crafting Your Blue-Ocean Value Proposition

Once you identify a promising niche, articulate a clear value proposition:

- **Target Audience**: Who exactly benefits?

- **Unique Challenge Addressed**: What gap do you fill?

- **Differentiating Features**: What methods, formats, or perspectives make your solution inimitable?

Frame this proposition in a single mission statement: "I empower [audience] to [transformation] through [unique method]," and use it as the north star for all content, partnerships, and product offerings.

Action Steps: Competitor Map; Blue-Ocean Brainstorming

Competitor Map (Mental or Visual)

1. **Axes Definition**

   - Choose two dimensions most relevant to your niche—such as "Depth of Expertise" vs. "Production Quality," or "Community Engagement" vs. "Topical Breadth."

2. **Plot Rivals**

   - Mentally (or on a whiteboard) position each rival creator according to these axes. Be candid: place fledgling channels closer to the origin and market leaders at the outer extremes.

3. **Identify Gaps**

   - Note the empty quadrants. Which intersections of expertise and quality remain unclaimed? Which competitive positions could yield high leverage with moderate effort?

4. **Assess Risks**

   - For each gap, consider barriers to entry—technical complexity, resource requirements, or audience adoption hurdles. Prioritize those openings where the barrier is surmountable yet few others are venturing.

Blue-Ocean Brainstorming (Guided Session)

1. **Gather Diverse Perspectives**

   - Invite team members, top fans, or industry peers to a brainstorming session. Machiavelli valued counsel from varied sources to avoid echo chambers.

2. **Warm-Up Exercises**

   o   Begin with "What-If" provocations: "What if our
       content were delivered entirely via audio drama?"
       or "What if we removed all spoken words and relied
       on data visualizations?" Encourage absurd ideas to
       spark creativity.

3. **Pain-Point Mining**

   o   List the top five complaints your audience
       voices—time constraints, jargon overload, lack of
       accountability—and brainstorm novel formats or
       partnerships that directly address each.

4. **Cross-Pollination**

   o   Assign each participant an unrelated
       domain—fashion, gaming, public speaking—and
       ask how its best practices could inform your niche.
       Then rotate groups to refine ideas.

5. **Idea Evaluation**

   o   For each concept, assess feasibility (resources,
       technical skill), desirability (audience appeal), and
       differentiation (competitive defensibility). Use
       simple scoring—high, medium, low—to build
       consensus.

6. **Prioritization and Next Steps**

- ○ Select the top two blue-ocean concepts. Draft a 30-day pilot plan for each, specifying content formats, launch channels, and success metrics. Assign owners and schedule check-ins.

By meticulously mapping rivals to unearth openings, rigorously applying SWOT analysis to your own strategy, and pursuing blue-ocean opportunities through structured brainstorming, you transform the chaotic battle for attention into a calculated campaign for authority. Just as Machiavelli's princes won dominions by knowing both themselves and their foes, you too will secure your principality in the digital realm—carving out spaces that no competitor has yet imagined, and fortifying them with your unique expertise and unwavering discipline.

Chapter 8: Resource Management

In *The Prince*, Machiavelli emphasizes that a ruler's success depends not only on bold strategy but on the prudent management of resources: men, money, and machines. He warns that "a prince ought to have no other aim or thought… than war, its organization, and discipline," yet immediately clarifies that "the levies of soldiers, the treaties with allies, and the fortresses that are built must all be subordinated to the fiscal health and administrative bandwidth of the state." For content creators, "war" is the ongoing campaign for audience attention, and the "state" is your brand ecosystem. You must budget time, tools, and talent as meticulously as Machiavelli's ideal prince guards his treasury. In this chapter, we break resource management into three pillars—time, tools, and team—show how to decide between outsourcing and building in-house capabilities, and map how to scale operations without sacrificing quality.

Time, Tools, and Team: Budgeting Your Resources Wisely

Machiavelli astutely observes that "one change always leaves open a road to others," implying that once you commit resources, your capacity to respond and adapt hinges on how you've allocated them. The triad of time, tools, and team forms the backbone of any sustainable content operation.

Time as Your Most Precious Asset

Time cannot be leveraged or invested—it only flows forward. Machiavelli reminds us that a wise prince "should not apply himself to any enterprise without considering how he will sustain it." For creators, sustaining a content strategy means realistic calendar planning that accounts for ideation, production, editing, promotion, and rest.

1. **Audit Your Current Time Allocation**
   Start by tracking every hour for one week: filming, scripting, editing, marketing, and administrative tasks. Machiavelli valued empirical observation; he urges princes to "study what actually happens, rather than what ought to happen in theory." Use this data to identify time sinks and opportunities for compression.

2. **Establish Core and Peripheral Activities**
   – **Core activities**: those that directly produce content—research, scripting, filming, editing.
   – **Peripheral activities**: social-media engagement, email management, bookkeeping.
   Assign fixed time blocks to core activities during your peak creative hours. Peripheral tasks can be batched into designated "administrative windows" to avoid context switching.

3. **Protect Focused Creation Blocks**
   Machiavelli warns that "he who neglects what is done for what ought to be done sooner effects his ruin." Guard your most fertile hours by using calendar tools to mark them as unavailable for meetings. Reserve those periods for deep

work, when interruptions are off-limits.

4. **Plan for Contingencies**
   Build "buffer days" into each content cycle. Unexpected delays—a sick day, a technical failure—should not derail your schedule. Machiavelli counsels that "fortune favors the prepared," and your calendar preparation should anticipate storms as well as fair weather.

Equipping Yourself with the Right Tools

Just as a prince's army marches most effectively with well-forged weapons and reliable supply lines, your creative production depends on the right mix of hardware and software. Yet Machiavelli cautions against overdependence on auxiliaries who serve only for pay; similarly, flashy tools that you neither master nor use regularly become liabilities.

1. **Inventory Existing Tools**
   List every piece of equipment (camera, microphone, lights), every software license (editing suites, graphic design platforms, analytics dashboards), and every service subscription (hosting, email automation). Evaluate each for frequency of use and impact on content quality.

2. **Prioritize Core Investments**
   Allocate budget first to those tools that deliver the greatest return on investment. A dependable microphone, for instance, often yields a more noticeable uptick in perceived professionalism than a midrange lens upgrade. Machiavelli's principle that "it is better to have few faithful

men than many mercenaries" applies: invest in a few essential, high-quality tools rather than a broad array of mediocre gadgets.

3. **Leverage Free and Open-Source Alternatives**
    Just as a prudent prince might conscript local levies instead of costly mercenaries, you can adopt open-source software—audio editors, design suites, project-management boards—that meets most needs without recurring fees. Test these options in parallel with premium tools before committing long-term.

4. **Regular Maintenance and Upgrades**
    Nothing derails production faster than outdated hardware or expired software. Machiavelli extols the virtues of regular inspections: "The prince who fortifies his city must often inspect its walls." Schedule quarterly audits of your toolset, applying firmware updates, retiring unsupported platforms, and reallocating budget toward emergent technologies.

Building and Nurturing Your Team

No prince rules alone. Machiavelli warns of the perils of relying solely on mercenaries: they serve only for coin and abandon the cause at the first opportunity. Instead, he recommends cultivating loyal citizens who share your vision. For a content creator, team members—whether employees, contractors, or volunteers—should align with your mission and enhance your capacity.

1. **Define Core Roles and Responsibilities**
   Identify the functions you cannot delegate—creative direction, on-camera presence, strategic planning—and those you can. Common roles include:

   - **Video Editor**

   - **Graphic Designer**

   - **Social Media Manager**

   - **Community Moderator**

   - **SEO Specialist**
     Craft clear job descriptions emphasizing outputs (e.g., "deliver 4 polished video edits per month") rather than inputs.

2. **Hire for Cultural and Mission Fit**
   Machiavelli prized virtù—character and capability—in his advisers. Seek team members who not only possess the technical skills you need, but who are motivated by your brand's purpose. In interviews, ask candidates to analyze your past content and suggest improvements; their answers reveal both competence and enthusiasm.

3. **Foster Loyalty Through Ownership**
   A prince secures loyalty by involving key figures in decision-making, granting them stakes in the realm's prosperity. Similarly, offer your team:

- ○ **Clear career paths**: outline progression from junior roles to senior leadership.

  ○ **Profit-sharing or bonuses**: tie rewards to channel growth milestones.

  ○ **Creative input**: invite ideas for series formats or campaign themes.
    When your collaborators feel invested, they champion your brand as fiercely as you do.

4. **Continuous Training and Development**
   Machiavelli's perfect prince never stops learning; he adapts to shifting military tactics and political currents. Likewise, invest in your team's growth—workshops on advanced editing techniques, SEO masterclasses, community-management certifications. A team that evolves with the landscape multiplies your capacity to respond and innovate.

Outsourcing vs. In-House: Freelancers, Agencies, and Interns

As Machiavelli distinguishes between unreliable mercenaries and loyal native troops, so must you choose between outsourcing tasks and nurturing in-house capabilities. Each model has trade-offs in cost, control, and scalability.

When to Outsource

1. **Specialized, Episodic Needs**
   Tasks that demand rare expertise—3D animation, advanced sound design, legal review—are often more cost-effective when outsourced. Engage freelancers or boutique agencies who charge premium rates but deliver high-impact results.

2. **Scalability for Short-Term Spikes**
   When launching a major campaign or product, you may need extra hands—graphic designers, copywriters, videographers—for a limited window. Short-term contracts avoid the overhead of permanent hires.

3. **Geographic and Cultural Diversity**
   Collaborating with creators or producers in different regions can infuse fresh perspectives and tap new markets. Outsourcing to international talent pools can also reduce costs while broadening your brand's global resonance.

Machiavellian Caution: Outsource only when you retain oversight. A prince who entrusts a fortress to mercenaries risks betrayal; similarly, overly opaque workflows lead to misaligned deliverables. Insist on regular check-ins, draft clear scopes of work, and maintain ownership of final assets.

When to Build In-House

1. **Core, Repetitive Functions**
   For work that underpins every piece of content—video editing templates, brand-consistent graphics, community moderation—it pays to develop in-house capacity. Over time, you'll achieve higher quality at lower incremental cost.

2. **Intellectual Property Protection**
   If you're creating proprietary processes or sensitive content—course curricula, proprietary frameworks—keep these within a trusted internal team to mitigate leaks or unauthorized use.

3. **Cultural Cohesion**
   An internal team, aligned day-to-day with your mission and brand voice, often produces more cohesive, consistent work than a rotating cast of freelancers. They internalize your style guide and brand values, reducing revision cycles.

Interns and Apprentices

Machiavelli's ideal state draws on the loyalty of citizens who see service as a pathway to honor. Interns—whether remunerated or through credit arrangements—can cultivate genuine allegiance while affording you enthusiastic support.

- **Clear Learning Objectives**: Offer structured mentorship, regular feedback, and project ownership.

- **Mutual Benefit**: Ensure interns gain portfolio-ready work and real-world skills; in return, you gain fresh energy and potentially long-term collaborators.

- **Supervision and Structure**: Prevent exploitation by assigning a dedicated mentor and setting realistic deliverables.

Scaling Content Operations Without Diluting Quality

Machiavelli warns that "the vulgar crowd always is taken by appearances"; if you scale too quickly and your output quality slips, your audience will notice the cracks in your facade. True expansion requires systems that preserve excellence even as volume increases.

Systematize Creative Workflows

1. **Documented Standard Operating Procedures (SOPs)**
   For every recurring process—video editing, thumbnail creation, social scheduling—draft step-by-step guides. A novice on your team should be able to follow the SOP and produce a publishable asset.

2. **Template Libraries**
   Develop branded templates for graphics, outlines for scripts, and presets for audio mixing. Machiavelli's court scribes used standardized seals and scripts; you too can optimize by reusing proven structures.

3. **Centralized Asset Management**
   Use a cloud-based repository where all raw footage, graphics, and project files are tagged by date, project, and status. This prevents duplication of effort and accelerates retrieval when repurposing old content.

Maintain Quality Through Rigorous Review

1. **Multi-Tiered Review Stages**
   Every piece of content should pass through at least two quality-control checkpoints: one for technical accuracy (audio levels, visual framing) and one for brand alignment (tone, messaging consistency).

2. **Feedback Loops**
   Encourage team members—and trusted beta viewers—to flag deviations from your style guide. Machiavelli prized frank counsel; cultivate a culture where critique serves the realm's strength.

3. **Performance Monitoring**
   Beyond initial publish metrics, track content longevity—evergreen views, continued engagement over months, referral traffic. If certain formats underperform,

revisit them before scaling further.

Phased Growth Strategies

1. **Pilot Programs**
   Before doubling your output, trial a single new format or additional upload day for one month. Assess resource strain, audience response, and ROI before committing to ongoing expansion.

2. **Staggered Role Expansion**
   Rather than hiring for five new positions at once, onboard one role, document the impact on team bandwidth and content performance, then proceed to the next. Machiavelli's incremental approach to conquest—securing one province before attacking the next—minimizes risk.

3. **Automate Routine Tasks**
   Employ automation for scheduling posts, aggregating analytics, and triggering simple audience interactions (welcome messages, re-engagement emails). Free your team to focus on high-value creative work.

Action Steps: Resource Allocation Worksheet; ROI Calculator

Resource Allocation Worksheet (Narrative Guide)

1. **List Your Resources**

   - Time: total available hours per week.

   - Tools: monthly and annual costs for each software and hardware item.

   - Team: roles, hourly rates or salaries, projected hours.

2. **Prioritize Activities**
   Rank tasks by impact on your key goals—audience growth, revenue, brand equity. Allocate resources starting from highest impact downward until you exhaust your budgeted hours and dollars.

3. **Set Allocation Targets**
   Assign percentage splits of time (e.g., 40% content creation, 20% editing, 15% promotion, 15% community engagement, 10% learning).

4. **Monitor and Adjust Monthly**
   At month's end, compare planned versus actual resource use. Where you overspent or underdelivered, investigate root causes and rebalance the next month's allocations.

ROI Calculator (Narrative Guide)

1. **Define Input Costs**
   Aggregate all expenses: team wages, tool subscriptions, equipment depreciation, and opportunity cost of your own hours (assign an hourly rate to your time).

2. **Measure Output Value**
   Assign monetary value to outcomes: ad revenue generated, sponsorship fees, product sales, affiliate commissions. Include proxy valuations for non-monetary benefits—email-list growth (e.g., average lifetime value per subscriber), brand partnerships unlocked, or high-profile speaking invitations.

3. **Calculate ROI**
   Use the formula:
   Return on Investment = (Total Value Generated – Total Costs) ÷ Total Costs

4. **Interpret Results**
   An ROI above 1.0 signals a net gain; below 0 indicates a net loss. Segment ROI by content pillar—evergreen tutorials, live streams, newsletters—to identify which resource allocations yield the highest returns.

5. **Inform Future Budgeting**
   Redirect resources toward high-ROI activities; experiment cautiously with low-ROI areas or revise their processes to improve efficiency.

By mastering the allocation of your most finite asset—time—investing wisely in tools, and cultivating a loyal, capable team, you mirror Machiavelli's model of disciplined statecraft. By choosing judiciously between outsourcing and building in-house capabilities, and by scaling methodically with robust workflows and quality checks, you ensure that every incremental expansion strengthens your principality—your brand—rather than diluting it. Armed with a living worksheet for resource allocation and an ROI calculator to measure impact, you stand ready to govern your creative realm with the strategic acumen of a true Machiavellian prince.

Chapter 9: Tactical Promotion and Distribution

In *The Prince*, Machiavelli teaches that "men in general judge more from appearances than from reality," and that "the vulgar crowd are taken by that which the eyes present to them, rather than by the things which are within." For the modern content creator, promotion and distribution are the vehicles by which your work appears before the eyes of your audience—shaping perception, sparking engagement, and cementing your authority. Yet the dilemma remains: how much to rely on organic momentum versus paid amplification, when to double down on one platform or withdraw, and how to wring every ounce of value from each piece of content by repurposing it across channels. In this chapter, we translate Machiavelli's counsel on prudent management, opportunistic timing, and resource maximization into an actionable playbook for tactical promotion.

Organic Reach vs. Paid Amplification

Machiavelli warns that reliance on mercenary forces brings danger: "he who depends entirely on good faith is often deceived," while "auxiliaries are useless and dangerous." In content marketing terms, organic reach is akin to citizen levies—genuine engagement born of loyal followers—whereas paid amplification functions like auxiliaries: hired troops you call in at need, powerful but potentially fickle if not managed wisely.

The Case for Organic Reach

1. **Sustainable Loyalty**
   Organic followers—those who subscribe, bookmark, and return—resemble the prince's faithful citizens more than fickle mercenaries. Their engagement arises from perceived value and emotional connection, making them more likely to share, recommend, and invest long-term in your offerings.

2. **Cost Efficiency**
   The upfront labor—SEO optimization, community engagement, collaboration with peers—yields compounding returns over time. Just as a fortified city requires initial construction but minimal upkeep, strong organic channels eventually broadcast your content with minimal additional expense.

3. **Authentic Signals to Algorithms**
   Platforms increasingly reward genuine interactions—comments, saves, watch time—over paid clicks. Machiavelli might liken this to how a prince's genuine acts of mercy earn deeper loyalty than mere bribery. Authentic engagement signals quality to algorithms, fueling further reach without extra budget.

The Role of Paid Amplification

1. **Immediate Impact**
   Paid ads, sponsored posts, and boosted content deliver predictable reach at scale—much as a prince might hire

mercenaries to defend or seize a key fortress. Use this power strategically: to announce launches, test new markets, or revive evergreen assets.

2. **Precision Targeting**
   Paid channels allow granular audience selection—geography, interests, behaviors—akin to how a savvy general spots the enemy's weakest flank. Targeted ads can place your work before high-value prospects who might never discover you otherwise.

3. **Control and Measurement**
   Unlike organic tactics, paid campaigns offer clear budgets, timelines, and ROI metrics. Machiavelli's ideal prince kept detailed ledgers of expenditure; likewise, run A/B tests on ad creative, copy, and placements to optimize spend and performance.

Balancing the Two

- **Foundation First**: Before pouring money into ads, ensure your organic engine runs smoothly: a well-optimized website, compelling lead magnets, engaged communities. Without a strong base, paid traffic will leak away without conversion.

- **Test and Scale**: Use small-budget paid experiments to validate messaging and audience segments. Once a campaign proves profitable, scale it gradually—just as Machiavelli advises expanding a principality one town at a time rather than risking all in a single siege.

- **Reinvest Wisely**: As paid efforts drive revenue, funnel a portion back into organic-building activities—such as content creation, SEO, and community programs—so that your reliance on external amplification diminishes over time.

Platforms Triage: When to Double Down or Pull Back

Machiavelli teaches that "fortune is a river which, when it overflows its banks, inundates the plains, but, when it retires, leaves the plains devastated and dry." Platforms, with their shifting algorithms and audience behaviors, can similarly swell and recede in opportunity. The key is to triage your presence—invest heavily where returns are rising, and redirect resources when signals warn of decline.

Identifying Growth Platforms

- **Rising Engagement Metrics**: Track week-over-week changes in reach, impressions, and interaction rates. A sudden uplift in response to new features (e.g., Reels on Instagram or Shorts on YouTube) signals a moment when doubling down will reap exponential dividends.

- **Early-Mover Advantage**: Platforms in nascent stages—Clubhouse's beta era, the early days of

TikTok—reward creators who join before saturation. Machiavelli admired princes who seized unguarded territories; similarly, staking your claim early can secure loyal followings before competition intensifies.

Recognizing Declining Channels

- **Stagnant or Dropping Metrics**: Consistent decreases in reach or engagement suggest the platform's algorithm no longer favors your content style. Continuing to post there is like maintaining a garrison in a fortress whose walls are crumbling.

- **Shifts in Demographics**: If your core audience migrates elsewhere—older viewers leaving Snapchat for Instagram, for instance—reevaluate where your efforts best serve both reach and resonance.

- **Platform Policy Risks**: Algorithm changes, ad policy shifts, or data-privacy reforms can suddenly throttle organic and paid performance. Machiavelli warned princes to guard against political tides; stay abreast of platform announcements to anticipate potential downturns.

Triage Framework

1. **Monthly Audit**: Review key metrics across all active channels. Score them on growth potential, audience fit, and strategic alignment.

2. **Resource Allocation**: Allocate 70% of your promotional budget (time + ad spend) to top-tier platforms, 20% to mid-tier experiments, and 10% to new or niche channels.

3. **Quarterly Pivot Points**: Every three months, reevaluate. If a mid-tier channel outperforms a top-tier one, bump its allocation upward. Conversely, trim resources from channels that consistently underdeliver.

4. **Exit Strategy**: For any channel you decide to deprioritize, plan a graceful withdrawal—announce reduced posting schedules, archive evergreen content, and guide followers toward your primary hubs.

Cross-Platform Repurposing: Maximizing ROI on Each Asset

Machiavelli extols efficiency: "A prince… who does not build keeps his rule precarious," but he also praises resourcefulness in using what one already possesses. For creators, each core content asset—an in-depth article, a long-form video, a podcast episode—represents a treasure trove of insights that, when repurposed strategically, can populate multiple channels with minimal extra effort.

Core-to-Micro Content Pipeline

1. **Pillar Asset Creation**

- Start with a comprehensive centerpiece: a 3,000-word blog post, a 45-minute webinar, or a 60-minute podcast. This "grand strategy" encapsulates your deepest expertise on one topic.

2. **Derivative Micro-Assets**

   - **Social Snippets**: Clip 30-second video highlights or pull compelling quotes for image posts.

   - **Audio Bites**: Extract 60-second audio teasers for platforms like Instagram Stories or Twitter.

   - **Infographics & Carousels**: Design visual summaries of key frameworks for LinkedIn or Pinterest.

   - **Email Nuggets**: Repurpose sections into a short newsletter series inviting readers to the full asset.

Benefits of Repurposing

- **Consistency of Message**: Like a prince stamping coinage with a uniform seal, using the same core insights across channels reinforces brand identity.

- **Cost Efficiency**: Once the pillar asset is produced, micro-assets require less time and budget, stretching your ROI further.

- **Algorithmic Favor**: Fresh posts featuring familiar foundational ideas signal relevance to both audiences and algorithms.

Ensuring Freshness

While repurposing leverages efficiency, Machiavelli warns against "taking up any other thing for his study" to the point of neglecting new content. Maintain a balance: for every five repurposed pieces, create at least one new pillar asset that pushes your brand forward.

Action Steps: Channel Decision Narrative; Repurposing Checklist

Channel Decision Narrative

1. **List Your Active Platforms**
   Note each channel where you publish: YouTube, Instagram, LinkedIn, TikTok, Twitter, email newsletter, podcast host, etc.

2. **Score Each on Three Axes**

   - **Reach Growth**: Are subscribers and impressions trending upward?

   - **Engagement Quality**: Are followers commenting, sharing, and converting?

  - **Strategic Fit**: Does this platform align with your brand voice and resource capacity?

3. **Allocate Your Effort**
   Assign relative percentages of your monthly promotion budget—both time and ad spend—to each platform based on scores.

4. **Set Review Milestones**
   Mark quarterly calendar reminders to reevaluate platform performance and adjust allocations.

Repurposing Checklist

- **Identify Pillar Assets**: Review your past three months of content; select your top three assets by performance or strategic importance.

- **Map Micro-Assets**: For each pillar, decide on:

  - Two 30-second video clips for social stories.

  - Three pull-quotes or data points for image posts.

  - One infographic summarizing the asset's main framework.

  - A 150–200 word excerpt for your newsletter.

- **Schedule Distribution**: Slot each micro-asset into your content calendar, ensuring that no two repurposed pieces from the same pillar drop in the same week.

- **Track Performance**: Monitor reach, engagement, and conversion of each micro-asset. Annotate which formats and platforms drive the best results for future planning.

By mastering the balance between organic growth and paid boost, by triaging your platform investments according to real-time signals, and by efficiently repurposing your core ideas across multiple channels, you execute a Machiavellian-grade campaign for attention. Each piece of content serves not merely as a singular dispatch but as a strategic asset in a broader arsenal—ensuring that your influence expands methodically, sustainably, and with maximum impact.

Chapter 10: Monetization and Revenue Streams

In *The Prince*, Machiavelli counsels that "a prince ought to have no other aim or thought… than war, its organization and discipline," for it is through prudent management of resources that a state endures. In the creator economy, monetization is your "war chest"—the financial foundation that sustains creativity, growth, and strategic freedom. In this chapter, we dissect direct and indirect revenue models, explore the nuances of subscriptions and memberships, unravel the psychology of pricing, and equip you with action-focused roadmaps to map and tier your income streams.

Direct vs. Indirect Models

Direct Models: Ads and Sponsorships
 Direct monetization resembles the taxes and tributes levied by princes on their domains. Machiavelli warns that "princes should avoid spoiling their subjects' property," yet he concedes that well-judged exactions—when proportional and predictable—provide necessary sustenance. In content terms, ads (pre-roll, display, or embedded) and sponsorships (branded integrations, shout-outs) are predictable, scalable, and often the first revenue many creators unlock.

- **Pros of Direct Models**

  1. **Immediate Feedback Loop:** View CPMs (cost per mille) and fill rates daily, adjusting your approach in real time.

  2. **Lower Barrier to Entry:** Platforms often enable ad revenue sharing with minimal application requirements.

  3. **Scalable with Traffic:** As your views climb, so too can your ad earnings—much like a prince whose land's tithe grows with population.

- **Cons of Direct Models**

  1. **Reliance on Platform Algorithms:** A sudden policy change or algorithmic tweak can slash ad rates overnight—akin to a rival prince diverting trade routes to deprive you of customs duties.

  2. **Viewer Friction:** Ads and sponsored segments can irritate audiences if overused or poorly integrated, risking erosion of goodwill.

  3. **Rate Volatility:** Advertisers may pause spending in economic downturns, mirroring Machiavelli's observation that "fortune is changeable," and revenues must be diversified.

Indirect Models: Merchandise, Courses, and Products
 Indirect monetization mirrors the creation of new industries and crafts within a principality—foundries, workshops, and toll roads—where princes can derive ongoing revenue without singling out citizens for heavier levies. Merchandise (branded apparel, prints), digital courses, ebooks, and physical products embody this principle.

- **Pros of Indirect Models**

    1. **Higher Margins:** Digital products often approach 90% gross margin once development is complete, unlike the 40–60% typical for ad revenue.

    2. **Brand Amplification:** Wearing your merch or taking your course turns customers into walking billboards—akin to citizens bearing your heraldic crest.

    3. **Audience Investment:** Purchasers of paid offerings have more "skin in the game," elevating their loyalty and lifetime value.

- **Cons of Indirect Models**

    1. **Upfront Effort:** Developing a flagship course or designing a quality merchandise line demands significant time and expertise—echoing Machiavelli's note that "new ordinances… cannot be established without sacrifice."

2. **Inventory and Fulfillment:** Physical products introduce logistical complexity and cost, requiring partnerships with manufacturers or print-on-demand services.

3. **Market Fit Risk:** Even the most polished product can flounder if it misreads audience needs, reflecting the dangers Machiavelli saw in over-extending resources on ill-judged conquests.

Strategic Blending of Direct and Indirect

Machiavelli extols the virtue of balancing multiple revenue sources: "Princes must estimate their expenses and revenues… and not depend on extraordinary exactions." For creators, a judicious mix—ads providing steady cash flow, sponsorships bridging peaks, and indirect products capturing high-margin transactions—creates a resilient income ecosystem.

1. **Core Funnel Structure:** Position ad revenue and sponsorships as top-of-funnel offerings—low commitment, broad reach—then nurture leads toward mid-funnel subscriptions and bottom-of-funnel flagship products.

2. **Revenue "Rungs":** Build ascending levels of engagement: free content → sponsored content → low-cost digital downloads → premium courses or merch bundles. Each rung primes audiences for the next.

3. **Dynamic Rebalancing:** Just as Machiavelli advises princes to augment or curb taxes based on public mood, monitor your revenue mix and recalibrate when one stream

By treating platform signals not as random noise but as intelligence reports, you anticipate shifts, allocate resources where they'll thrive, and guard against being blindsided by policy or algorithmic upheavals.

Pivot Frameworks: When and How to Change Direction

Machiavelli observes that "fortune is changeable, and people do not keep faith with one who seems unprepared for adversity." A creator who refuses to adapt risks obsolescence; one who masters the art of the pivot harnesses change as an engine of growth. But pivots must be strategic, not frantic. Below is a framework to judge both the timing and method of your directional shifts.

1. **Establish Clear Pivot Triggers**

   - Define quantitative thresholds—90-day declines of more than 15% in key metrics, subscriber growth below a baseline, or ad revenue contraction over consecutive months. These triggers prevent emotional or opportunistic pivots, anchoring decisions in data. Machiavelli prized measurable counsel over rash impulse: "He who acts contrary to advice runs the risk of failing."

2. **Diagnose Root Causes**

   - Before pivoting, ask: is the issue format-specific (e.g., my livestreams lag behind pre-recorded videos)? Platform-specific (my podcast downloads are fine, but video views slump)? Or content-specific (my topic no longer resonates)? Conduct A/B tests, survey your audience, and review competitive benchmarks to isolate the precise levers you must adjust.

3. **Define Pivot Scope**

   - **Incremental Pivots** adjust existing formats—shortening intros, swapping thumbnail styles, or shifting posting days.

   - **Transformative Pivots** overhaul your approach—launching a new series, exploring a fresh niche, or adopting a wholly different medium (audio, text, or live).
     Machiavelli admired decisive governors who knew when to enact sweeping reforms and when to tinker at the margins: "One must wisely discern whether to bear the old mischief or remedy it by introducing a new one."

4. **Pilot in Controlled Environments**

   - Rather than flipping your entire publishing calendar overnight, run small-scale pilots. Reserve a secondary channel or a less-trafficked slot for experimental content. Gauge response, refine your method, then scale. This "test, learn, scale" cycle mirrors Machiavelli's recommendation to secure footholds before committing full forces to a risky campaign.

5. **Communicate with Your Audience**

   - Abrupt changes can alienate loyal viewers. Preempt confusion with transparent messaging: "Starting next month, I'll be focusing on short-form tutorials! Here's why I believe you'll love this new format…" When Machiavelli's prince introduced new taxes, he first prepared the people with explanations about necessity and benefit; likewise, warm up your community to forthcoming changes to maintain trust.

6. **Iterate Rapidly and Document**

   - Track each pivot's planning, execution, and outcomes in a living playbook. Document what worked, what backfired, and which audience segments responded best. Over time, you'll build a repertoire of proven pivot strategies to draw upon—an internal arsenal of battle plans for future shifts.

By embedding pivot frameworks into your strategic rhythm, you transform platform volatility from a threat into a source of competitive advantage—ensuring your content remains vital, your tactics current, and your brand ever resilient.

Building Redundancy: Diversifying Content and Income

Machiavelli understood that a single fortress, however strong, could fall if besieged. He advised rulers to fortify multiple strongholds, cultivate alliances, and avoid dependence on any one node of power. For creators, redundancy means diversifying both content formats and revenue streams so that if one channel falters, the others sustain your momentum and livelihood.

1. **Content Format Diversification**

   - **Core Pillar Content:** Maintain your flagship series—long-form videos, in-depth articles, or full-length podcasts—that anchor your brand identity.

   - **Supplementary Formats:** Explore micro-content—short-form clips, infographics, or email newsletters—that engage audiences in different contexts (scrolling feeds, commuting, casual browsing).

   - **Emergent Mediums:** Experiment with live audio, VR experiences, or interactive webinars to future-proof your portfolio. Machiavelli would applaud a ruler who spreads his influence across land, sea, and air; you too should span formats to cover every corner of your audience's consumption habits.

2. **Platform Layering**

   - Build a presence on at least three distinct platforms with non-overlapping algorithmic logics—e.g., YouTube for search-driven video, Instagram for visual storytelling, and an email list for direct audience access. Each platform becomes a bulwark, so that algorithmic shifts on one don't sink your entire enterprise.

3. **Revenue Stream Redundancy**

   - **Ad and Sponsorship Revenue:** The traditional levies that fill your treasury day by day.

   - **Digital Products and Courses:** High-margin offerings that convert at launch events and drip passive sales long-term.

   - **Memberships and Subscriptions:** Recurring pledges that smooth cash flow and strengthen community loyalty.

   - **Merchandise and Physical Goods:** Branded assets that diversify income and deepen brand embodiment.

- o **Affiliate and Licensing Partnerships:** Leverage your audience to generate commissions or royalty income.
  Machiavelli cautioned that "emperors who relied solely on the 'fortunate' tribute of gold mines and taxes found their states vulnerable when sources dried up." By building multiple, independent revenue pillars, you fortify yourself against any one stream drying up.

4. **Cross-Training Your Skills**

   - o Invest time in learning adjacent disciplines—audio engineering, basic graphic design, copywriting—so that you're never wholly reliant on a single specialist. Should your editor depart or a supplier fold, you possess the competence to maintain minimum viable operations until new talent can be recruited.

5. **Financial Reserves and Budget Buffers**

   - o Maintain a cash reserve sufficient to cover at least six months of operating expenses. Machiavelli revered the prince who stored grain and coin against famine; by saving during prosperous times, you shield your creative principality from dry spells when views or sales contract.

Through redundant layers—of content, platforms, revenue, and skills—you create a resilient ecosystem where failure in one domain triggers no existential crisis, but rather signals an opportunity to lean into alternative strengths.

Action Steps: Scenario Planning; Stress-Test Your Strategy

To ensure that your adaptation and resilience practices aren't mere theory, you need concrete exercises that simulate challenges, reveal weaknesses, and prepare your team for rapid, confident responses.

1. Scenario Planning Workshop

- **Assemble Your Council:** Bring together your core team—editors, marketers, community leads—for a two-hour intensive session.

- **Define Critical Uncertainties:** Identify two key variables with the most disruptive potential: e.g., "Major ad policy change on Platform X" and "Sponsorship market downturn."

- **Draft Four Scenarios:** Combine high/low permutations of each variable to create scenarios such as "Ad rates halve, but sponsorships soar," or "Both ad rates and sponsorship budgets plummet."

- **Strategize Responses:** For each scenario, sketch immediate actions—budget reallocations, content format shifts, membership drives—and longer-term strategies—new product development, platform migration, talent hiring.

- **Assign Ownership:** Designate who leads each response plan, with clear roles and timelines.

2. Stress-Test Your Content Engine

- **Simulated Platform Outage:** For one week, treat your primary channel as if it's offline. Re-route all promotional efforts to secondary platforms. Document friction points: missing workflows, knowledge gaps, or technical blockers.

- **Revenue Shock Drill:** Model a sudden 30% drop in your top revenue stream. Activate your redundancy plans—promote alternative products, launch a flash sale, accelerate affiliate campaigns—and record time to recovery and effectiveness of each tactic.

- **Team Role Redundancy Test:** Have team members temporarily swap roles (editor becomes community manager, and vice versa) for a day. Observe handoff challenges and document cross-training needs.

3. Quarterly Resilience Review

- Schedule a standing quarterly meeting to revisit pivot triggers, platform audits, revenue diversification metrics, and scenario plans. Update each plan with new data, retire outdated contingencies, and refine emerging best practices.

4. Living Resilience Dashboard

- Maintain a real-time dashboard (simple spreadsheet or project-management board) tracking:

    - Engagement velocity by platform

    - Revenue distribution across streams

    - Status of scenario plans ("green" for tested, "yellow" for partial, "red" for untested)

    - Cash reserve levels relative to burn rate

- Use this dashboard in every leadership huddle to detect drift and ensure your operation remains battle-ready.

By mastering the art of reading platform signals, deploying disciplined pivot frameworks, building redundancy across every facet of your ecosystem, and rigorously stress-testing your strategy through scenario planning and drills, you internalize Machiavelli's enduring lesson: that true strength lies not in resisting change, but in orchestrating it to your advantage. With adaptation and resilience as your guiding maxims, your creator principality stands prepared to weather any storm—emerging not only unshaken, but stronger and more influential than before.

Chapter 12: Legacy and Long-Term Influence

In *The Prince*, Machiavelli reminds rulers that true power endures beyond the span of a single reign. He writes, "He who establishes himself on new modes and institutions must look with special care to one thing alone, and that is to strengthen his power." As a content creator, you are building more than a channel or a following—you're crafting a legacy, a body of work and an ecosystem that can outlast platform changes, personal pivots, and even your own tenure. This chapter explores the avenues of thought leadership, the responsibilities of mentorship and stewardship, and the practicalities of crafting an exit strategy—whether passing the torch to trusted hands, selling your brand, or gracefully retiring.

Thought Leadership: Writing Books, Speaking Engagements, and Courses

Machiavelli secured his own legacy through the enduring power of his writings. Likewise, as a creator your deepest insights deserve permanence in books, signature courses, and the lecture halls of live events.

- **Writing a Book:**
  A well-crafted book cements your authority in ways ephemeral social posts cannot. Begin by mapping a clear

thesis—your unique philosophy on your niche—and outline chapters that translate your most impactful content into structured, enduring narrative. Engage professional editors, invest in thoughtful cover design, and plan launch events that harness your community's momentum. Each book sold becomes both revenue and a testament to your expertise, carried onto shelves and e-readers long after algorithms forget your latest post.

- **Securing Speaking Engagements:**
  Public speaking elevates your profile among peers and opens doors to new audiences. Cultivate signature talks—a 20-minute keynote, a 45-minute workshop—with polished slide decks and compelling anecdotes. Apply to industry conferences, pitch corporate retreats, or host your own salon gatherings. As Machiavelli noted that princes "must make a name as generous and munificent" before they can command esteem, your speaking presence does the same: it demonstrates mastery and generosity of insight, inviting invitations rather than forcing them.

- **Designing Flagship Courses:**
  Courses represent the apex of packaged expertise. Structure them like Machiavelli's treatises: clear, modular, and actionable. Introduce foundational principles, illustrate with historical or modern case studies, and assign real-world exercises. Offer live Q&A sessions, peer reviews, and certification badges. Thoughtfully priced and rigorously delivered, your course becomes both a learning vehicle and a brand ambassador—students carry your methods into their own worlds, extending your influence

exponentially.

By investing in these pillars—print, stage, and classroom—you ensure that your ideas ripple outward and endure, long after ephemeral trends have faded.

Mentorship and Community Stewardship

Machiavelli underscores that a prince's subjects form the bedrock of his rule: "Men are driven rather by fear than by love…" but the wisest provokes affection through benevolence. As your following matures, stewardship shifts from mere content delivery to active mentorship and community care.

- **Building a Mentee Program:**
  Identify your most promising followers—those who demonstrate initiative, passion, and alignment with your values. Structure a formal program: quarterly cohorts of five to ten mentees who work through a guided curriculum, attend monthly roundtables, and receive one-on-one feedback. Provide them project briefs that mirror professional scenarios, invite them into strategy sessions, and help them launch their own niche projects.

- **Empowering Community Leaders:**
  As Machiavelli counseled princes to build alliances with local lords, empower long-time community members to serve as ambassadors. Offer them moderator roles, special badges, or "advisor" titles. In exchange, solicit their

insights into emerging trends, and involve them in
beta-testing new content. Their enthusiasm and grassroots
reach amplify your message and foster organic growth.

- **Hosting Mastermind Retreats:**
  Once or twice a year, convene a select group—top
  mentees, high-tier subscribers, fellow creators—for
  multi-day retreats. These intimate gatherings combine
  workshops, strategy deep-dives, and social rituals that
  strengthen bonds. Machiavelli's courts thrived on such
  exclusive ceremonies; your mastermind becomes a
  crucible for collaboration, innovation, and enduring loyalty.

Through dedicated mentorship and thoughtful stewardship, you
transform passive audiences into active allies—ensuring that your
work sparks further creation and community long after a single
video or post fades.

Preparing Exit Strategies: Selling, Handing Off, or Retiring Your Brand

No reign lasts forever, and wise princes plan for succession.
Similarly, content creators must envision an exit—whether
monetizing the brand, passing it to protégés, or winding down
gracefully.

- **Selling Your Brand:**
  If your content empire garners consistent revenue and
  houses valuable intellectual property, you may attract

acquisition offers. Prepare by maintaining clean financials—revenue reports, subscriber growth metrics, and a catalog of courses, trademarks, and domain assets. Engage legal counsel to draft clear asset purchase agreements. A successful sale transfers your brand's goodwill to a new steward, rewarding you for years of labor and securing the brand's continuity.

- **Handing Off to Proteges:**
  If you wish your vision to persist, identify and groom successors—perhaps top mentees or community leaders. Codify your brand style, workflows, and institutional knowledge into comprehensive manuals. Gradually transfer responsibilities—content planning, team management, sponsor relationships—while overseeing quality. Machiavelli's ideal succession avoided jarring power vacuums; your phased handover ensures fans witness a seamless transition rather than an abrupt departure.

- **Retiring with Dignity:**
  If you choose to conclude your content journey, craft a farewell arc: a series of reflective content pieces that celebrate milestones, share lessons learned, and express gratitude. Offer final "legacy" products—complete archives, 'best of' anthologies, or commemorative digital booklets. Encourage your community to carry forward the ethos you built. Machiavelli warns princes against departing in weakness; retire with a clear, celebratory crescendo that honors both your work and your audience.

Planning your exit—be it sale, succession, or retirement—ensures that the value you cultivated endures and that your final acts reinforce, rather than diminish, the legacy you leave behind.

Action Steps: Legacy Blueprint; Mentee Program Outline

Legacy Blueprint

1. **Define Enduring Contributions:** List three signature works (book, course series, flagship event) that encapsulate your core philosophy.

2. **Map Distribution Channels:** Ensure each work resides in robust formats and platforms—print, evergreen course platforms, recorded keynote libraries.

3. **Document Institutional Knowledge:** Create a "Creator's Bible" covering workflows, brand voice guidelines, sponsor contacts, and community protocols.

4. **Outline Succession Paths:** Identify potential successors, draft handover timelines, and schedule mentorship milestones.

5. **Set Exit Milestones:** Establish financial and creative goals that trigger exit phases—e.g., "Upon reaching $X in passive course sales, begin succession mentorship."

Mentee Program Outline

1. **Selection Criteria:** Define eligibility—engagement levels, content skills, alignment with brand values.

2. **Curriculum Modules:**

   - Module 1: Niche Refinement and Authority Building

   - Module 2: Content Strategy and Production Workflows

   - Module 3: Community Engagement and Monetization

   - Module 4: Leadership and Legacy Planning

3. **Engagement Cadence:** Weekly group calls, bi-weekly one-on-one sessions, and monthly guest expert workshops.

4. **Project Assignments:** Real-world briefs—launch a mini-series, design a membership tier, host a live event—with feedback loops and peer review.

5. **Graduation Criteria:** Completion of capstone projects, demonstration of audience growth metrics, and contribution to the community knowledge base.

By investing in thought leadership, nurturing mentorship pathways, and planning your eventual exit, you transform your creator journey into a principality that lives on—empowering others, shaping industries, and leaving a legacy that resonates long after any single post or platform has passed. As Machiavelli's enduring works continue to influence centuries later, so too can your body of work inspire and guide generations of creators to come.

Conclusion and Next Steps

As we reach the final pages of **Lessons from The Prince: Content Creators**, it's time to gather the threads of Machiavellian wisdom and weave them into your own strategic tapestry. This conclusion serves three purposes: it distills the core lessons you've absorbed, it equips you with a personal "Prince's Plan" template to chart your next moves, and it inspires you to maintain momentum through ongoing reflection and adaptation.

Review of Core Lessons

Over the past twelve chapters, we've recast Machiavelli's treatise on power into the language of likes, shares, and subscriptions. Here's a distilled tour of the principles you've mastered:

1. **Establish Your Domain**

   - Machiavelli: "A prince ought to have no other aim or thought… but war and its organization and discipline."

   - Modern Equivalent: Define your niche narrowly, consolidate your focus, and draw clear territorial lines in the digital landscape so that every piece of content reinforces your claim.

2. **Build and Maintain Authority**

   - Machiavelli: "It is better to be feared than loved, if you cannot be both."

   - Modern Equivalent: Cultivate respect through consistent quality, strategic vulnerability, and principled stances rather than chasing fleeting popularity.

3. **Forge Alliances and Networks**

   - Machiavelli: "He who relies entirely on good faith is often deceived."

   - Modern Equivalent: Enter collaborations with clear terms, preserve your autonomy, and turn critics into allies through strategic generosity.

4. **Manage Perception**

   - Machiavelli: "Men judge generally more by the eye than by the hand."

   - Modern Equivalent: Harmonize authenticity and aspiration in your persona, maintain visual consistency, and spin your narrative to position every release as part of a grander saga.

5. **Guard Your Reputation**

   - Machiavelli: "The vulgar crowd always is taken by appearances."

   - Modern Equivalent: Use praise, blame, and selective disclosure to sculpt your public image; harness testimonials, reviews, and user-generated content as social proof; respond to crises with either apology or pivot.

6. **Surprise and Innovate**

   - Machiavelli: "Whosoever desires constant success must change his conduct with the times."

   - Modern Equivalent: Embrace viral pivots, time your bold experiments in harmony with platform tides, and A/B test relentlessly to balance novelty with familiarity.

7. **Analyze Competition**

   - Machiavelli: "If an enterprise is difficult, men will more readily attempt it if it seems possible to achieve by their own exertions."

   - Modern Equivalent: Map rivals' strengths and weaknesses, conduct SWOT analyses, and hunt for blue-ocean niches where competition is minimal.

8. **Manage Resources**

   - Machiavelli: "Princes must estimate their expenses and revenues."

   - Modern Equivalent: Budget your time, tools, and team; decide when to outsource versus build in-house; scale carefully through SOPs and quality checks.

9. **Promote Tactically**

   - Machiavelli: "Men in general judge more from appearances than from reality."

   - Modern Equivalent: Balance organic reach with paid amplification, triage platforms based on real-time signals, and repurpose every pillar asset to maximize ROI.

10. **Monetize Strategically**

- Machiavelli: "There is no method of avoiding the need for tribute… but prudence will enable the prince to minimize it."

- Modern Equivalent: Blend direct ads and sponsorships with high-margin indirect products; structure subscriptions and memberships with tiered value; wield pricing psychology to align fees with perceived worth.

11. **Adapt and Endure**

- Machiavelli: "Fortune favors the bold, but she yields to the prepared."

- Modern Equivalent: Read algorithmic shifts as intelligence signals, pivot with clear frameworks, build redundancy across content and income streams, and stress-test your strategy to withstand shocks.

12. **Craft a Lasting Legacy**

- Machiavelli: "Men are driven rather by fear than by love… but the prudent prince blends both."

- Modern Equivalent: Cement thought leadership through books, courses, and keynotes; mentor rising creators; and plan for an exit that preserves and extends your brand's influence.

Creating Your Personal "Prince's Plan"

All these lessons converge in one decisive document: **Your Prince's Plan**. This living blueprint transforms lofty ideas into a granular roadmap of strategy, actions, and checkpoints. Use the following template as a scaffold—customize each section to your ambitions, resources, and timeline.

1. **Vision & Mission Statement**

   - **Vision:** A concise declaration of the world you aim to shape with your content.

   - **Mission:** The specific approach you'll take to realize that vision, anchored in your niche and unique strengths.

2. **Strategic Pillars** (Select up to four)

   - Authority Building

   - Network & Alliances

   - Innovation & Surprise

   - Resource Mastery

   - Platform Dominance

   - Revenue Diversification

   - Legacy & Mentorship

3. **Quarterly Objectives**
   For each of the next four quarters:

   - **Objective:** What you aim to achieve (e.g., "Grow email list by 25%," "Launch paid mastermind," "Hit 100K YouTube subscribers").

- **Key Results:** Two or three metrics that quantify success.

- **Major Initiatives:** The high-level projects you'll undertake (new series, book launch, platform expansion).

4. **Monthly Action Plans**
   Break each quarterly initiative into monthly tasks with owners, deadlines, and estimated resource commitments. Identify any dependencies—like "Finalize guest list before webinar recording."

5. **Weekly Check-In Questions**

   - Which metric shifted most this week, and why?

   - Did we test any new hypothesis? What did we learn?

   - Which pillar received less attention than planned? How will we rebalance?

6. **Risk & Contingency Log**
   For each major objective, note potential threats (platform deprecation, sponsor withdrawal, personal bandwidth limits) and backup plans (alternate channels, reserve funds, delegation strategies).

7. **Reflection & Adaptation Space**
   A dedicated section to capture qualitative insights: audience feedback highlights, surprising industry

developments, and personal growth milestones.

Staying the Course

Machiavelli reminds us: "Men in general judge more by the eye than by the hand, for everyone sees what you appear to be, but few know what you really are." Your audience will judge your commitment by the cadence of your efforts, the consistency of your values, and the authenticity of your journey. To stay the course:

- **Embrace Small Victories:** Regularly celebrate incremental wins—your first 10 new subscribers after a pivot, a positive review, a successful collaboration. These moments fuel momentum.

- **Honor Your Commitments:** If you pledge a weekly livestream, deliver it—even when inspiration wanes. Your reliability cements trust far more than a burst of sporadic brilliance.

- **Guard Against Burnout:** Machiavelli counseled princes to balance austerity with humane treatment of their subjects. Similarly, schedule rest, delegate tasks that drain you, and invest in practices that replenish your creativity.

- **Periodically Revisit Your Plan:** At least once per quarter, step back to ask: Are my objectives still aligned with my vision? Has the landscape shifted in ways that demand revision?

Final Reflective Prompts for Vision and Mission Alignment

Use these prompts at the close of each planning cycle to ensure that every tactic, every campaign, and every product remains true to your core purpose:

1. **Impact Check:** In what tangible ways did my content improve the lives or knowledge of my audience this period?

2. **Integrity Audit:** Which actions felt most aligned with my values? Which moments tempted me to compromise, and how did I respond?

3. **Forward Momentum:** What is one bold experiment I can introduce next quarter that stretches my comfort zone but serves my mission?

4. **Community Insight:** What new patterns are emerging in audience feedback, and how will I integrate these insights?

5. **Legacy Lens:** Which piece of work this year do I want remembered a decade from now, and what steps will I take to preserve and amplify it?

As Machiavelli concludes his treatise by reminding princes that "fortune is dynamic, and to master her one must adapt swiftly," so do you end this book armed not with static doctrines but with actionable frameworks. Your mission from this point forward is clear: review the core lessons, draft your Prince's Plan, commit to disciplined execution, and keep your gaze fixed on the horizon of growth and influence. With strategy as your compass and action as your means, you stand ready to rule your creative realm with wisdom, resilience, and the enduring power of a true content prince.

THIS IS NOT A COLLECTION

This volume is part of **Ancient Wisdom Hacks**—
an ongoing body of work focused on how strategy, power, and
failure actually function under pressure.

The books are only one layer.

What you are reading is an entry point into a larger system of
interpretation, application, and expansion.

WHAT THESE WORKS ARE DESIGNED TO DO

Most people look for answers.

These works expose patterns:

- How decisions are made before they are visible
- How systems weaken before they collapse
- How power shifts before it is recognized

This is not theory.
It is applied observation.

THE SYSTEM BEHIND THE WORK

Across all volumes and future releases, three forces remain
constant:

- **Strategy** — how outcomes are shaped before action
- **Conflict** — how people and systems break under pressure
- **Power** — how control is gained, maintained, and lost

No single book contains the full picture.
Each adds another angle.

CONTINUE BEYOND THIS VOLUME

New interpretations, applied volumes, and extended works are
released continuously.

To access current and future material, visit:

www.AncientWisdomHacks.com

WHAT YOU WILL FIND

- Additional applied volumes across industries
- Expanded interpretations of foundational texts
- New releases not available through standard distribution
- Future projects extending beyond books

The system is still expanding.

FINAL POSITION

Clarity does not make outcomes easier.

It removes the illusion that they were ever simple.

Ancient Wisdom Hacks
Interpretation over repetition.
Application over theory.

underperforms or risks audience fatigue.

Subscriptions, Memberships, and Patreon Mechanics

Machiavelli wrote that "he who becomes prince through the favour of the people ought to keep them friendly by satisfying them." Subscriptions and memberships are the digital parallel: recurring commitments through platforms like Patreon, Substack, or YouTube Memberships bind your most devoted supporters in mutually beneficial pacts.

Defining Your Membership Value

1. **Exclusive Content:** Early access videos, bonus episodes, or members-only livestreams. Machiavelli would recognize these as "privileges" granted to your inner circle—symbols of status that cost little to produce but yield high perceived value.

2. **Community Access:** Private Discord channels, monthly Q&A sessions, or live workshops. These gatherings echo the princely courts where trusted advisors conferred—strengthening loyalty through participation.

3. **Physical Tokens:** Branded stickers, hand-signed notes, or small merch drops. Machiavelli praised material gifts for securing allegiance; a timely physical package can delight

members and deepen emotional bonds.

Tier Structures and Mechanics

- **Entry Tier (Low commitment):** $3–$5/month. Includes access to a private feed and occasional shout-outs.

- **Mid Tier (Core supporters):** $10–$20/month. Adds behind-the-scenes content and monthly AMAs.

- **Premium Tier (Power users):** $50–$100/month. Offers 1:1 calls, quarterly merch, and input into content roadmaps.

Machiavelli cautions that "it is necessary for a prince to know how to feign goodness… and to be a great pretender." In modern terms, your tier names, descriptions, and benefit framing shape perceived value. Label your mid-tier "Council of Champions," your premium tier "Founders' Circle," evoking exclusivity and honor.

Platform-Specific Mechanics

- **Patreon:** Built-in tier flexibility, patron management, and integrated messaging. Take advantage of "Goals" to gamify member acquisition: "At 200 patrons, I'll release a special mini-series."

- **Substack:** Emphasizes newsletter content and paywalls. Ideal if written essays are your forte. Use "free + paid" model to maximize list growth then convert top 10% into subscribers.

- **YouTube Memberships:** Embeds directly in your channel, delivering badges, emojis, and members-only live chat. Leverage your regular videos to call out membership perks.

Retention and Upsell Strategies
Machiavelli reminds us that "men are moved more by fear than by love." For memberships, craft gentle urgency—limited-time merch add-ons for new subscribers, annual renewals with price guarantees—to nudge renewals. Simultaneously, cultivate "love" through consistently delivering promised perks and surprising members with unannounced bonuses.

Pricing Psychology: Fees, Tiers, and Perceived Value

"A prince ought to appear merciful, faithful, humane, upright, and religious," Machiavelli notes—not necessarily to possess all those virtues, but to project them. Pricing operates similarly: the numerical cost you present must align with the value you project to justify it.

Anchoring and Contrast
Present a high-anchor price alongside your intended price to elevate its appeal. If your flagship course costs $499, place it next to an "All-Access Pass" at $999. By contrast, $499 seems like a bargain—even if it's still a premium offering. Machiavelli would

applaud this tactic as a form of "feigned generosity": you frame your true ask in the light of an even larger figure.

Charm Pricing vs. Rounded Figures

- **Charm Pricing:** $19.99 feels psychologically cheaper than $20.00. It speaks to precision and research.

- **Rounded Figures:** $200 signals simplicity and quality. It appeals to segments who associate round numbers with ease and prestige.

Choose your approach based on audience sophistication. Machiavelli understood that "the vulgar crowd always is taken by appearances," whereas seasoned nobles judge by substance. Similarly, a budget-minded demographic responds to charm pricing, while corporate clients expect round numbers.

Price Tiers and Decoy Options
Offer three tiers: Basic, Standard, and Premium. Position the middle option as your "sweet spot" by making the Basic too sparse and the Premium significantly more expensive—nudging most buyers toward Standard. This decoy effect mirrors Machiavelli's strategic positioning: guiding subjects to the choice you most desire without overt coercion.

Perceived Value through Payment Structures

- **One-Time Fees:** Ideal for courses—upfront investment conveys depth and finality.

- **Installment Plans:** Spread payments over three or six months, reducing friction for high-ticket items but increasing perceived total cost.

- **Subscription Pricing:** Lower monthly fees create ongoing revenue and perceived affordability, as labor pain is distributed over time. Machiavelli would recognize this as a form of "incremental tribute"—manageable exactions that avoid rebellion.

Value Stacking and Bonuses
 Include limited-edition bonuses—live workshops, private consultations, or exclusive tools—for early birds or first-week purchasers. Machiavelli believed in rewarding early supporters to cement alliances before opponents can mobilize. Similarly, "early bird" bonuses convert on-the-fence prospects by adding urgency and value.

Action Steps: Monetization Roadmap; Pricing Tier Worksheet

1. Monetization Roadmap (Narrative Guide)

- **Phase 1: Foundation**

    - Audit existing audiences and engagement channels.

- Identify current revenue streams and quantify monthly income.

  - Set short-term goals: e.g., "Increase ad revenue by 20% in six months."

- **Phase 2: Diversification**

  - Launch one indirect product: a mini-course or digital download tested with your top-engaged segment.

  - Initiate a Patreon or membership tier with clear perks.

  - Negotiate two new sponsorships aligned with your brand values.

- **Phase 3: Optimization**

  - A/B test price points across tiers and payment structures for new offerings.

  - Refine messaging, anchoring, and bundle composition based on conversion data.

  - Automate recurring billing, product delivery, and member onboarding workflows.

- **Phase 4: Scaling**

- Expand product catalog: develop advanced courses or premium mastermind groups.

- Increase ad budgets for best-performing campaigns.

- Explore affiliate or licensing partnerships to extend reach without overhead.

2. Pricing Tier Worksheet (Narrative Guide)

- **Define Tier Names and Positioning**

  - Tier 1: [Name]—Entry-level, core offering, priced at $X. Communicates accessibility.

  - Tier 2: [Name]—Flagship package with key bonuses, priced at $Y. Framed as best value.

  - Tier 3: [Name]—Elite experience with VIP perks, priced at $Z. Signals exclusivity.

- **List Included Benefits**

  - For each tier, bullet the deliverables—courses, community access, 1:1 calls, merch. Ensure each ascending tier adds distinct, high-value items.

- **Set Price Anchors**

    - Identify an "anchor" (unofficial MSRP) higher than Tier 3 to establish value perception.

    - Position Tier 2 relative to this anchor to maximize perceived discount.

- **Outline Payment Options**

    - Offer one-time payment and installment plans. Note the total cost difference and friction trade-offs.

    - Decide on subscription vs. perpetual access structures.

- **Map Launch Timing**

    - Establish launch windows and bonuses for early adopters.

    - Schedule scarcity triggers—limited seats or expiration dates—to drive timely action.

By weaving direct revenue streams with high-margin indirect offerings, crafting subscription and membership structures that mirror Machiavelli's lessons on loyalty and privilege, and applying pricing psychology that balances anchoring, tier strategy, and perceived value, you build a monetization engine both robust and agile. Armed with a clear roadmap and a detailed tier worksheet, you transform your creative principality into a sustainable enterprise—one capable of funding your vision, rewarding your community, and outlasting the vicissitudes of algorithmic fortune.

Chapter 11: Adaptation and Resilience

In *The Prince*, Machiavelli teaches that "whosoever desires constant success must change his conduct with the times." No ruler endures by rigidly clinging to yesterday's playbook; rather, he reads the ebb and flow of fortune, seizes new opportunities, and fortifies his state against unforeseen storms. For the modern content creator, adaptation and resilience are not optional virtues but survival imperatives. Platforms evolve, audience tastes shift, and what once delivered explosive growth can overnight become outdated. In this chapter, we explore how to read platform signals and algorithm shifts, deploy pivot frameworks that determine when and how to change course, build redundancy through diversified content and revenue channels, and—finally—equip yourself with actionable scenario planning and stress-testing exercises to ensure your strategy endures any tempest.

Reading Platform Signals and Algorithm Shifts

Machiavelli likened fortune to a river: when it swells, it inundates the plains; when it recedes, it leaves the fields parched. Likewise, algorithmic tides on YouTube, Instagram, TikTok, and other platforms can either carry your content to new heights or strand it in obscurity. A shrewd prince studies weather patterns to time his military campaigns; a shrewd creator monitors platform signals to time launches, diversify formats, and safeguard reach.

1. **Monitor Engagement Velocity**

   o Track the rate at which new followers arrive, how quickly view counts climb in the first 24 hours, and the acceleration or deceleration of shares and saves. A sudden spike in early engagement often signals algorithmic favor—akin to breezes filling a ship's sails—while a plateau or decline warns that your content may be slipping from the platform's recommendation loops.

2. **Interpret Feature Rollouts**

   o Each new tool—Reels, Stories, Shorts, Live Rooms—represents a strategic opening. When a platform promotes a beta feature, it often boosts early adopters to incentivize usage. Recall that Machiavelli counseled princes to "strike while the iron is hot"; join nascent features swiftly, but do so judiciously—test with low-stakes content before retooling your entire strategy around an unproven format.

3. **Listen to Official Communications**

   o Platforms frequently announce policy or algorithm changes via blogs, newsletters, and developer conferences. Treat these as unclassified directives from the prince's council: read them thoroughly, discuss implications with your team, and adjust your roadmap to comply with new guidelines or exploit emerging priorities—whether that means favoring video over still images, longer sessions over clicks, or vice versa.

4. **Leverage Community Intelligence**

   - Creators share observations and data leaks in forums, Discord servers, and private Slack groups. While rumors must be vetted, a consensus among experienced users about shifting metrics—such as "Engagement rate now outweighs follower count"—can guide your next moves. Machiavelli prized counsel from diverse voices; assemble a small advisory panel of trusted peers who can surface anomalies or confirm industry gossip.

5. **Analyze Cross-Platform Patterns**

   - If your Instagram Stories engagement dips while your TikTok duet requests surge, the discrepancy suggests where to invest your energy. Map which formats consistently outperform others across channels. This mosaic of insights replaces guesswork with evidence-based direction—ensuring that when one platform's tide recedes, you pivot to another whose currents still run strong.